450

Y0-BCV-076

RIDE THE EAST WIND

RIDE THE EAST WIND

EAST WIND

Parables of Yesterday and Today

EDMUND C. BERKELEY

Quadrangle/The New York Times Book Company

I am deeply indebted to the creative men and women from 3500 B.C. to A.D. 1973 whose thoughts and work it has been my great privilege to present in this book.

E.C.B.

Copyright © 1973 by Edmund C. Berkeley

All rights reserved, including the right to reproduce this book or portions thereof in any form. For information, address: Quadrangle/The New York Times Book Company, 10 East 53 Street, New York, New York, 10022. Manufactured in the United States of America. Published simultaneously in Canada by Fitzhenry & Whiteside, Ltd., Toronto.

Library of Congress Catalog Card Number: 73-82477

International Standard Book Number: 0-8129-0375-7

Design by Tere LoPrete

Acknowledgments

The author is grateful to the following:

"The Elephant and the Donkey: A Fable" by James Reston © 1972 by The New York Times Company. Reprinted by permission.

"Much Obliged, Dear Lord" copyright 1952 by Fulton Oursler from *Modern Parables* by Fulton Oursler. Reprinted by permission of Doubleday & Co., Inc.

"The Differences in Two Strains of Corn" from *Plants, Man and Life* by Edgar Anderson, second edition published by the University of California Press, reprinted by permission of The Regents of the University of California.

"The First Climbing of the Highest Mountain in the World," portion by Sir John Hunt: From *The Conquest of Everest* by Sir John Hunt. Copyright 1953 by Sir John Hunt. Published by E. P. Dutton & Co., Inc., and used with their permission. Also from *The Ascent of Everest* by Sir John Hunt and used by permission of the publishers, Hodder & Stoughton. Copyright.

Dugald Stewart Walker's two illustrations for *The Garden of Paradise* were originally published by Doubleday, Page & Co. in 1914, in a book *Andersen's Fairy Tales* which contained twelve of his tales, and a great many illustrations and decorations by Walker.

Percy J. Billinghurst's illustrations originally appeared in *A Hundred Fables of Aesop* from the English version of Sir Roger L'Estrange published by John Lane, the Bodley Head, London and New York, in 1903. These illustrations are "The Crow and the Fox," "The Lion in Love," "The Crow and the Mussel," "The Crow and the Pitcher," "The Lark and Her Young Ones," "The Wasps and the Honey Pot," and "The Fox and the Grapes."

The author wishes to thank the following young illustrators, who in 1973 lived in or near Boston: Susan Bard, for "The Two Raccoons and the Button"; Michael J. Errato for ". . . there used to be a cornfield"; Diane Bowden for "The Peddler and the Peachtree," "The Swirl of Rose Petals," and the bouquet symbols used in this work; Janice Kolagic for "The Fly, the Spider and the Hornet," "The Elephant on a Barrel," "The Sighting of a Whale," "The Stars and the Young Rabbit," and "The New-fangled Warning System."

I also acknowledge with warm gratitude the help I received from Pamela Allison, Zinaida Alexi, Douglas Levene, Ned McLeroy, and Herbert Nagourney who provided comments, protests, suggestions, and good ideas about some versions of my parables, and so persuaded me or prodded me to produce better versions.

Contents

VII. PROBLEM SOLVING

Introduction

This book is a collection of over 50 parables (including anecdotes, allegories, and fables) by more than 20 authors, both modern and ancient. These parables have been selected with a purpose: to throw light on some famous problems, modern, classic, or ageless, through the medium of stories either fictional or true.

Many of these parables are decorated by a "bouquet" of proverbs, quotations, and remarks rather than a single moral. A simple example of a bouquet is "The early bird gets the worm" followed by "Look what the worm got for being early." In this way it is easier to make clear the many-sided nature of truth and to avoid the simplistic single moral of bygone days. Besides, most good stories imply more than one conclusion.

 This is the symbol for a bouquet of remarks quoted from the parable: a collection of noteworthy things said. These remarks are likely to be on different subjects. This symbol has a name, "bouq-rem."

 This is the symbol for a bouquet of morals, maxims, conclusions, and quotations from famous men or nonfamous men, where the idea or ideas of the parable are commented on cogently. This symbol has a name, "bouq-mor."

This is the symbol for an analysis of the situation discussed in the parable, the response to the question "What is the analysis of this problem and its solution?" This symbol has a name, "bouq-anal."

What makes a parable?

On the obvious first level, a parable is a story. As a story, it has a setting, characters, a plot, a narrative, suspense, a climax. When the story has been told well, it has unity, coherence, emphasis, is thoroughly entertaining, and is so vivid that it is almost unforgettable. Aesop would never have been a great success if he had not told excellent stories.

A parable has a second level, an underneath level, an implied level. This level consists of the principle or set of principles of which the story is an example or illustration.

In the past, four words have been used for what we here are calling a "parable." These four words are: parable (with a more limited meaning, often referring to the Bible), allegory, fable (with emphasis on brevity), and anecdote (for use only when the story is true).

To report properly on common sense and wisdom, however, requires using true stories as well as fictional stories, long stories as well as short ones. This too has been recognized. For example, there is the anecdote of Diogenes, who using a lighted lantern in the daytime, searched in the streets of Athens for an honest man and found none. This anecdote we would classify here as a parable.

In situations that occur frequently a story with fictional characters and events can ring true. In situations that occur rarely, only stories based on events that have actually or very probably happened, seem to be convincing: "Truth is stranger than fiction."

This book arises as a part of a current widespread reaction to the extraordinary tide of scientific advance and technological change which has taken place from the time of the beginning of World War I to the war in Indochina. In general, for about sixty years, people everywhere have been concentrating on the fantastic innovations of modern science and technology, such as radio, television, air travel, nuclear energy, computers, antibiotics, and so on. The subject matter of common sense, wisdom, and virtue has seemed "not relevant" or as if it could be assumed or expected.

That tide is now changing; perhaps it is even starting to ebb. Many people have newly become aware of the closed cycle of the environment of the planet Earth that surrounds us. We are noticing the population explosion, "limits to growth," the side-effects of thoughtless technology. There are limits to the severe changes that the Earth can accept from man. Many of us have come to suspect that if we are not more careful about the side-effects of the changes we are producing, it is likely that man will become extinct within the next few hundred years.

To avoid this danger, to deal with these newly seen problems, one of the sensible things to do is to study common sense and wisdom recorded in the past, especially what bears on the problem of truth, the nature of common sense, and the pursuit of wisdom and virtue.

Some of the common sense and wisdom to be searched for is in parables. A parable like an Aesop fable invites rather than compels a reader to acquire more common sense and wisdom. And if we had more of those capacities, we could avoid many more mistakes than we do avoid—and we could live much happier and more satisfactory lives.

Newtonville, Mass.
August, 1973

EDMUND C. BERKELEY

Part 1

THE
CONDITION
OF
MAN

Pandora and the Mysterious Box

H. A. GUERBER

The first mortals lived on earth in a state of perfect innocence and bliss. The air was pure and balmy; the sun shone brightly all the year; the earth brought forth delicious fruit in abundance; and beautiful, fragrant flowers bloomed everywhere. Man was content. Extreme cold, hunger, sickness, and death were unknown. Jupiter, who justly ascribed a good part of this beatific condition to the gift of heavenly fire conferred by Prometheus, was greatly displeased, and tried to devise some means to punish mankind for the acceptance of the heavenly fire.

With this purpose in view, he assembled the gods on Mount Olympus, where, in solemn council, they decided to create woman; and, as soon as she had been artfully fashioned, each one endowed her with some special charm, to make her more attractive. Their united efforts were crowned with the utmost success. Nothing was lacking, except a name for the peerless creature; and the gods, after due consideration, decreed she should be called Pandora. Then they bade Mercury take her to Prometheus as a gift from heaven; but he, knowing only too well that nothing good would come to him from the gods, refused to accept her, and cautioned his brother Epimetheus to follow his example. Unfortunately Epimetheus was of a confiding disposition, and when he beheld the maiden he exclaimed, "Surely so beautiful and gentle a being can bring no evil!" and accepted her most joyfully.

The first days of their union were spent in blissful wanderings, hand in hand, under the cool forest shade; in weaving garlands of fragrant flowers; and in refreshing themselves with the luscious fruit, which hung so temptingly within reach.

One lovely evening, while dancing on the green, they saw Mercury, Jupiter's messenger, coming towards them. His step was slow and weary, his garments dusty and travel-stained, and he seemed almost to stagger beneath the weight of a huge box that rested upon his shoulders. Pandora immediately ceased dancing, to speculate with feminine curiosity upon the contents of the chest. She nudged Epimetheus, and in a whisper begged him to ask Mercury what brought him thither. Epimetheus complied with her request; but Mercury evaded the question, asked permission to deposit his burden in their dwelling for safekeeping, professing himself too weary to convey it to its destination that day, and promised to call for it shortly. The permission was promptly granted. Mercury, with a sigh of relief, placed the box in one corner, and then departed, refusing all hospitable offers of rest and refreshment.

He had scarcely crossed the threshold, when Pandora expressed a strong desire to have a peep at the contents of the mysterious box; but Epimetheus, surprised and shocked, told her that her curiosity was unseemly, and then, to dispel the frown and pout seen for the first time on the fair face of his beloved, he entreated her to come out into the fresh air and join in the merry games of their companions. For the first time, also, Pandora refused to comply with his request. Dismayed, and very much discouraged, Epimetheus sauntered out alone, thinking she would soon join him, and perhaps by some caress atone for her present willfulness.

Left alone with the mysterious casket, Pandora became more and more inquisitive. Stealthily she drew near, and examined it with great interest, for it was curiously wrought of dark wood, and surmounted by a delicately carved head, of such fine workmanship that it seemed to smile and encourage her. Around the box a glittering golden cord was wound, and fastened on top in an intricate knot. Pandora, who prided herself specially on her deft fingers, felt sure she could unfasten it, and, reasoning that it would not be indiscreet to untie it if she did not raise the lid, she set to work. Long she strove, but all in vain. Ever and anon the laughing voices of Epimetheus and his companions, playing in the luxuriant shade, were wafted in on the summer breeze. Repeatedly she heard them call, and beseech her to join them; yet she persisted in her attempt. She was just on the point of giving it up in despair, when suddenly the refractory knot yielded to her fumbling fingers, and the cord, unrolling, dropped on the floor.

Pandora had repeatedly fancied that sounds like whispers issued from the box. The noise now seemed to increase, and she breathlessly applied her ear to the lid to ascertain whether it really proceeded from within. Imagine, therefore, her surprise when she distinctly heard these words, uttered in the most pitiful accents: "Pandora, dear Pandora, have pity upon us! Free us from this gloomy prison! Open, open, we beseech you!"

Pandora's heart beat so fast and loud, that it seemed for a moment to drown all other sounds. Should she open the box? Just then a familiar step outside made her start guiltily. Epimetheus was coming, and she knew he would urge her again to come out, and would prevent the gratification of her curiosity. Precipitately, therefore, she raised the lid to have one little peep before he came in.

Now, Jupiter had malignantly crammed into this box all the diseases, sorrows, vices, and crimes that afflict poor humanity; and the box was no sooner opened, than all the ills of man flew out, in the guise of horrid little brown-winged creatures, closely resembling moths. These little insects fluttered about, alighting, some upon Epimetheus, who had just entered, and some upon Pandora, pricking and stinging them most unmercifully. Then they flew out through the open door and windows, and fastened upon the merrymakers without, whose shouts of joy were soon changed into wails of pain and anguish.

Epimetheus and Pandora had never before experienced the faintest sensation of pain or anger; but, as soon as these winged evil spirits had stung them, they began to weep, and alas! quarreled for the first time in their lives. Epimetheus reproached his wife in bitterest terms for her thoughtless action; but in the very midst of his vituperation he suddenly heard a sweet little voice entreat for freedom. The sound proceeded from the unfortunate box, whose cover Pandora had dropped in the first moment of her surprise and pain. It pleaded, "Open, open, and I will heal your wounds! Please let me out!"

The tearful couple viewed each other inquiringly, and listened again. Once more they heard the same pitiful accents; and Epimetheus bade his wife open the box and set the speaker free, adding that she had already done so much harm by her ill-fated curiosity, that it would be difficult to add materially to its evil consequences; and that, perchance, the box contained some good spirit, whose ministrations might prove beneficial.

It was well for Pandora that she opened the box a second time, for the gods, with a sudden impulse of compassion, had concealed among the evil spirits one kindly creature, Hope, whose mission was to heal the wounds inflicted by her fellow-prisoners.

Lightly fluttering hither and thither on her snowy pinions, Hope touched the punctured places on Pandora's and Epimetheus'

creamy skin, and relieved their suffering, then quickly flew out of
the open window, to perform the same gentle office for the other
victims, and cheer their downcast spirits.

Thus, according to the ancients, evil entered into the world,
bringing untold misery; but Hope followed closely in its footsteps,
to aid struggling humanity, and point to a happier future.

Trouble and I are never far apart.

—*H. Addis, 1943*

A clever man turns great troubles into little ones, and little ones
into none at all.

—*Chinese proverb*

This I know full well—if all men should take their private troubles
to market, for barter with their neighbors, not one but when
he had looked into the troubles of other men would be right
glad to carry home again what he had brought.

—*Herodotus, c. 445* B.C.

Man has no other possession but Hope.

—*Thomas Carlyle, 1834*

You must hope for the best.

—*Cicero, 46* B.C.

There is more delight in hope than in enjoyment.

—*Japanese proverb*

Hope is a slender reed for a stout man to lean on.

—*T. C. Haliburton, 1843*

The Garden of Paradise

HANS CHRISTIAN ANDERSEN

Once upon a time there was a King's son. Nobody had so many or
such beautiful books as he had. He could read about everything

that had ever happened in this world, and see it all portrayed in really beautiful pictures. He could find out information about every land and every people; but where the Garden of Paradise was to be found not a single word could he discover. And this was the very thing that he thought about unendingly.

When he was very little and was just starting to school, his grandmother told him that every flower in the Garden of Paradise was a delicious cake, and that the centers of the flowers contained the choicest wine. In one flower, history was written, and in another flower, geography, and in a third flower, arithmetic; so that one only had to eat the cake, and one knew the lesson; and the more cake one ate, the more history, geography, and arithmetic one learned.

All this he believed at the time; but as he became a bigger boy, and learned more, and became wiser, he could see that the delights and splendors of the Garden of Paradise had to be far beyond all this.

"Oh, why did Eve take of the Tree of Knowledge? Why did Adam eat of the forbidden fruit? If I had been he, it would never have happened—then sin would never have come into the world."

This is what he said then, and he still said it when he was seventeen years old; and his thoughts remained full of the Garden of Paradise.

One day he walked into the woods. He was walking quite alone, for that was his greatest pleasure. The evening came, the clouds gathered, and rain streamed down as if the heavens had become one single river from which water poured; it became as dark as night in the deepest well. Often he slipped on smooth wet grass; often he fell over smooth wet stones, which jutted out of the rocky ground. Everything was soaked with water, and there was not a dry thread on the Prince. He had to climb over great blocks of stone where water gushed out of thick moss. He was almost worn out—but then he heard a strange murmuring, and saw before him a vast, lighted cave. In the middle of it burned a great fire, and on the fire a splendid stag with great antlers was being roasted on a spit, and was turning slowly between two felled pine trunks. An elderly woman, large, strongly built, looking almost like a man in disguise, sat by the fire, throwing logs on from time to time.

"Come in!" she called to the Prince. "Sit down by the fire and dry your clothes."

"There is a tremendous draft here," said the Prince, as he sat down on the ground by the fire.

"It will be worse than this when my sons come home," said the Woman. "You are in the Cavern of the Winds; my sons are the four Winds of the world. Do you understand that?"

"Where are your sons?"

"It is difficult to answer when stupid questions are asked," said the Woman. "My sons do as they like and go where they please. Right now they are bowling with the clouds up yonder in the King's hall," and she pointed upwards to the sky.

"Oh!" said the Prince. "You seem to speak gruffly; you are not so gentle and mild as the women I usually see around me."

"Yes, most likely they have nothing else to do. But I must be harsh and stern if I am to keep my sons under control. But I can do it though they are an obstinate lot. Do you see those four bags hanging on the wall? They are just as frightened of them as you used to be of the cane kept behind the hall mirror. I can fold up any one of the boys, I can tell you, and then he has to go into the bag; there is no ceremony about it; and there he has to stay; he can't get out to play tricks again until I think fit to allow him. But here comes one of my sons."

The North Wind rushed in with piercing cold; great hailstones skipped about on the floor; snowflakes fell. He was dressed in trousers and jacket of bearskin; a cap of sealskin was drawn down over his ears; long icicles hung from his beard; one hailstone after another dropped from the collar of his jacket.

"Don't go straight to the fire," said the Prince. "You might harm your frostbitten hands and face."

"Frostbitten," said the North Wind, with a loud laugh. "Frost is my greatest delight. What sort of a delicate traveler are you? How did you find your way into the Cavern of the Winds?"

"He is my guest," said the old Woman, "and if you are not pleased with that explanation, you may go into the bag! Do you understand that?"

The North Wind calmed down, and now told where he came from and where he had been for the past month.

"I come from the Arctic seas," he said. "I have been in the icy land of the polar bear with the walrus hunters. I sat at the helm and slept when they sailed from the North Cape. When I awoke now and then, the stormy petrels were flying around my legs. They are queer birds; they give a brisk flap of their wings, then hold them quite motionless, yet dart along at full speed."

"Don't be too long-winded," said the Mother of the Winds. "So at last you came to Behring Island?"

"It's beautiful there. There's a floor for dancing as flat as a pancake, with half-thawed snow, a little moss, sharp stones, and the bones of walruses and polar bears; it looked like the arms and legs of giants covered with rusty green. One would think the sun never shone there. I blew a little upon the mist so that one could see a shed; it was a house built of driftwood and covered with walrus skins—the fleshy side turned outwards. It was all red and green. On the roof sat a live polar bear growling.

"I went to the shore and looked at birds' nests, and saw the unfledged nestlings screaming and gaping; I blew down thousands of their throats, and taught them to shut their mouths. Farther on huge walruses were splashing about like monster maggots with pigs' heads and teeth a yard long."

"You tell your story well, my son," said the old Woman. "It makes my mouth water to hear you."

"Then the walrus hunters began hunting. The harpoons were hurled into the breasts of the walruses, so that smoking streams of blood spurted like fountains over the ice. Then I remembered my part of the sport. I blew up a storm; I made my ships, the mountain-high icebergs, crush the boats. Oh, how the hunters whistled and screamed and cried, but I whistled and screamed louder than they. They were obliged to throw the walrus carcasses, their chests, their ropes and tackle, out upon the ice. I shook heaps of snowflakes over them and let them drift south in their crushed boats to taste the salt water. They will never come again to kill walruses on Behring Island."

"Then you have been doing evil," said the Mother of the Winds.

"What good I have done, others may tell you," replied he. "But here comes my brother from the west. I like him best of all; he smells of the sea, and brings a splendid coolness with him."

"Is that little Zephyr?" asked the Prince.

"Yes, certainly, he is Zephyr," replied the old Woman. "But he is no longer little. Years ago he was a pretty boy, but that's gone by."

The West Wind looked like a wild man of the woods; he was

wearing a padded hat so as not to come to harm. He carried a great club of mahogany, hewn in the mahogany forests of America. It was no plaything.

"Where do you come from?" asked his Mother.

"From the forest wildernesses," he said, "where the thorny creepers make fences between the trees, where the watersnakes lie in the wet grass, and where people are not needed."

"What did you do there?"

"I looked into the deepest river; I watched how it rushed down over rocks, and turned into spray, and shot up towards the clouds to carry the rainbow. I saw the wild buffalo swimming in the river, but the river carried him off course; he floated with the wild ducks. They soared into the sky as they came to cataracts; but the buffalo was carried over the falls. That pleased me, and I blew up a storm, so that ancient trees were whirled about like match sticks."

"And have you done anything else?" asked the old Woman.

"I have been turning somersaults in the grasslands. I have stroked the wild horses. I have shaken the coconut palms. Yes, I have stories in plenty to tell. But one need not tell all one knows. You know that well, Mother."

And he kissed the old Woman so roughly that she nearly fell over; he was indeed a wild boy.

The South Wind came into the cave now, wearing a turban and a flowing Bedouin cloak.

"It's fearfully cold in here," he cried, and threw some more wood on the fire. "It is easy to tell that the North Wind arrived here first."

"It's hot enough here to roast a polar bear," growled the North Wind.

"You're a polar bear yourself," retorted the South Wind.

"Do you want to be put into the bag?" said the old Woman. "Sit upon that stone over there and tell me where you have been."

"In Africa, Mother," he answered. "I have been hunting lions with the Hottentots in the land of the Kaffirs. Grass grows there in those plains as green as an olive tree. There the ostriches ran races with me, but I am swifter than they.

"I went into the desert with its yellow sand. It looks like the bottom of the sea. I found a caravan. The travelers were killing one of their last camels to get water to drink, but they got very little. The sun was burning above them, and the sand was burning below them. Endless desert stretched far and wide around them. Then I rolled in the fine loose sand, and whirled it up into great pillars of sand storms. You should have seen how the camels stood terrified and the merchants drew their caftans over their heads. They threw themselves down before me as if I had been Allah, their God. Now they are buried—dunes of sand cover them all. Some day when I blow the dunes away, the sun will bleach their bones white; then other travelers may see that men have been there before them. Otherwise, no one would believe that in the desert."

"So you have done nothing but evil," exclaimed the Mother of the Winds. And before the South Wind was aware of it, she had seized him around his body, and stuffed him into a bag. He rolled around upon the floor of the cave, but she sat down on the bag, and that kept him still.

"Those are spirited sons of yours," said the Prince.

"Yes," the old Woman replied, "but I know how to control them. Here comes the fourth boy."

The East Wind came in dressed like a Chinese.

"Oh, have you come from that direction?" said his mother. "I thought you had been in the Garden of Paradise."

"I don't fly there till tomorrow," said the East Wind. "It will be a hundred years tomorrow since I was there. I have just come from China, where I danced around the porcelain tower till all the bells rang and rang again: 'Tsing, tsang, tsu.' In the streets the officials were being flogged, and bamboo canes were being broken over their shoulders. Yet they were officials from the first to the ninth rank. They cried aloud, "Many thanks, father and benefactor," but they didn't mean what they said. And I kept on ringing the bells which sang 'Tsing, tsang, tsu.' "

"You are foolish about it," said the old Woman. "It is a good thing that you are going to the Garden of Paradise tomorrow; it always helps in your education. Mind you drink deeply out of the spring of wisdom, and be sure to bring home a little bottleful for me."

"That I will do," said the East Wind. "But why have you clapped my brother the South Wind into the bag? I need him out. He must tell me about the Phoenix, for the Princess in the Garden of Paradise always wants to hear about that bird, when I pay my visit every hundredth year. Open the bag, please. Then you

The eagle in the great forest flew swiftly, but the Eastwind flew
more swiftly still

will be my sweetest of mothers, and I will give you two pockets-
ful of tea, as green and fresh as when I plucked it where it grew."

"Well, for the sake of the tea, and because you are my dear
boy," said the old Woman, "I will open the bag."

She did so and the South Wind crept out, but he was quite
crestfallen because the strange Prince had seen his disgrace.

"Here is a palm leaf for the Princess," said the South Wind.
"This palm leaf was given to me by the Phoenix; there is only one
such bird in the whole world. With his beak he has scratched
upon the leaf a description of all the hundred years that he has
lived. Now she may read how the Phoenix set fire to its nest himself and sat on it while it burned, like the funeral pyre of a Hindu
widow. How the dry branches crackled! What a smoke there was!
At last it all burst into flame and the old Phoenix was burned to
ashes, but its egg lay glowing in the fire. Finally the egg broke with
a loud bang, and the young Phoenix flew out. The young Phoenix
is now ruler over all the birds and it is the only Phoenix in the
world. It has bitten a hole in the leaf I gave you. That is its greet-
ing to the Princess."

"Let's have something to eat now," said the Mother of the
Winds; and they all sat by the fire to eat the roasted stag. The
Prince sat by the side of the East Wind, and they soon became
good friends.

"Tell me," said the Prince, "who is this Princess about whom
there is so much talk? What is the way to the Garden of Paradise?"

"Oh ho!" said the East Wind. "Do you want to go there? Well
then, fly tomorrow with me. But I must warn you that no man has
been there since the time of Adam and Eve. You have read of
them in your Bible histories?"

"Yes," said the Prince.

"When Adam and Eve were driven out of the Garden of Eden,
which is the same as the Garden of Paradise, it sank into the
earth; but it kept its warm sunshine, its mild air, and all its splendors and charms. The Queen of the Fairies lives there; and there
lies the Island of Bliss, where death never comes, and where living is a perpetual delight, and everything is beautiful. You may
ride on my back tomorrow, and I will take you with me; I think it

can be managed. But now let's leave off talking, for I want to sleep."

In the early morning the Prince awoke, and he was astonished to find himself high above the clouds. He was sitting on the back of the East Wind, held securely. They were so high in the air that the woods and fields, the rivers and lakes, looked as if they had been painted on a map unrolling below them.

"Good morning," said the East Wind. "You might very well sleep a little longer for there is not much to see in the flat country under us, unless you would like to count the churches. They stand like dots of chalk on a green carpet."

"It was rude of me not to say good-bye to your mother and your brothers," said the Prince.

"When one is asleep, one is excused," replied the East Wind.

They flew faster than ever. One could hear the East Wind and the Prince in the tops of the trees, for when they passed, the leaves and twigs rustled; one could hear them on the seas and the lakes, for when they passed, the water rose higher and the great ships bowed themselves toward the water like swimming swans.

Towards evening when it became dark, the great towns looked as if they were sprinkled with jewels, with their lights twinkling here and there. The Prince applauded, clapping his hands, but the East Wind told him he had better use his hands to hold fast, for otherwise he might fall and get caught on a church steeple.

The eagle in the great forest flew swiftly, but the East Wind flew more swiftly still. The Cossack on his horse sped fast over the plains, but the Prince sped faster still.

"Now you can see the Himalayas," said the East Wind. "This is the highest mountain range in Asia. Now we shall soon reach the Garden of Paradise."

They turned more to the south, and soon the air became fragrant with flowers and spices; figs and pomegranates grew wild, and wild vines bore clusters of red grapes and purple grapes. Here they both alighted, and stretched themselves on soft grass, where flowers nodded to the wind as if to say "Welcome!"

"Are we now in the Garden of Paradise?" asked the Prince.

"Not at all," said the East Wind, "but we shall soon get there. Do you see that wall of rock and the great cave over there, where wild vines cluster making a green curtain? Through there we shall pass. Wrap yourself up in your cloak. Here the sun is scorching, but a step inside the cave it will be icy cold. If a bird hovers at the entrance of the cave, it has one wing in summer heat, and the other wing in wintry cold."

"So that is the way to the Garden of Paradise!" remarked the Prince.

They proceeded into the cave. Oh, how icy cold it was in there —but this did not last long. The East Wind spread out his wings, and they gleamed like the brightest flame.

What a cave it was! Great blocks of stone, from which water dripped, hung overhead in extraordinary shapes. Sometimes the passage was so narrow, they had to creep on their hands and knees. At other times the passage was as wide and lofty as if they were in the open air. The cave looked like a vast chapel of the dead with silent organ pipes.

"Are we passing through the road of Death to the Garden of Paradise?" inquired the Prince. But the East Wind did not answer a word, but simply pointed forward to where beautiful blue light was shining.

The stone blocks over their heads became more and more like mist, and at last became as transparent as a white cloud in the moonlight. The air became deliciously mild, as fresh as on hilltops, and as fragrant as among roses.

A river ran there as clear as the air itself, and the fishes were like silver and gold. Purple eels flashed blue sparks at every moment as they curved and played in the water. The broad leaves of water lilies were tinged with all the hues of the rainbow; the flowers of the water lilies were like orange flames, nourished by the water in the same way as a lamp flame is nourished by oil.

Ahead of them, a delicate yet firm bridge of marble, so lightly built that it looked as if made of lace and glass beads, led them across the water to the Island of Bliss where the Garden of Paradise bloomed.

Were these palm trees or giant water-plants growing here? The Prince had never before seen such verdant, mighty trees. The most wonderful climbing vines hung on them in wreaths such as are only to be found illuminated in gold and colors in the margins of old books of the Saints, or entwined among the initial letters of chapters. Here was the most extraordinary combination of birds and flowers and scrolls.

Close by on the grass stood what seemed to be a flock of peacocks with their brilliant starry tails outspread. Yet when the Prince touched them, he found that they were not birds but plants, great burdock leaves looking and shining like peacocks' tails.

The lion and the tiger sprang like agile cats among the green bushes, which were as fragrant as the blossoms of the olive tree. And the lion and the tiger were tame. The wild wood-pigeon, glistening like a beautiful pearl, beat on the lion's mane with his wings; and the antelope, ordinarily so shy, stood close by, nodding, as if he wished to join in the playing.

The Fairy of the Garden of Paradise now appeared and came forward to greet the Prince and the East Wind. Her garments shone like the sun, and her face was as joyful as the face of a mother when she is happy and rejoicing over her child. The Fairy was young and very beautiful, and she was accompanied by a band of pretty maidens, each with a gleaming star in her hair.

When the East Wind gave her the inscribed leaf brought from the Phoenix, her eyes shone with pleasure.

She took the Prince's hand, and led him into her palace, where the walls were the color of the brightest tulips when they are held up in the sunlight. The ceiling was one great shining flower, and the longer one gazed into it, the deeper the flower cup appeared to be.

The Prince went to a window, and looked through one of the panes. Here he saw the Tree of Knowledge, and the Serpent, and Adam and Eve, moving as if they were all alive.

"Were they not driven out from the Garden of Eden?" he asked.

The Fairy smiled and explained to him that Time had burned that picture into the pane, but not as people are accustomed to see pictures, still and unmoving. No, there was motion in that picture: the leaves of the trees moved, and people moved too.

Then the Prince looked through another pane, and he saw Jacob's dream with the ladder reaching up to heaven, and angels with great wings ascending and descending.

Yes, everything that had happened in the world continued to live and move in these panes; such cunning pictures only Time could record.

The Fairy smiled at the Prince's astonishment, and led him into a great lofty hall, whose walls appeared transparent. Here were portraits of people, and each face looked fairer and more charming and he drank. He felt more joy than he had ever known before. He saw the background of the hall open, and there the Tree of Knowledge stood in a radiance which was almost blinding. The singing was as soft and lovely as his mother's voice; and it was as if he were a child, and his mother were singing "My child, my beloved child."

Then the Fairy beckoned to him, and said to him, so tenderly and sweetly and charmingly, "Come with me!" that he rushed towards her, forgetting at the moment his promise, his resolution, everything—this on the very first evening that she smiled and beckoned to him. And still she beckoned and smiled.

The fragrance in the scented air grew stronger; the harps sounded more lovely than ever; and it seemed as if the millions of smiling heads in the hall where the Tree of Knowledge grew sang and nodded "One must know everything. Man is the lord of the earth."

Looking at the Tree of Knowledge, he thought that these were no longer drops of blood that the Tree of Knowledge wept; instead it seemed to him that they were red shining stars.

"Come with me, come with me," the quivering voice of the Fairy still cried. At every step towards her, the Prince's cheeks burnt hotter and hotter, and his blood coursed more and more rapidly.

Remembering now the Fairy's earlier command, the Prince said to himself, "I will go. It is no sin to see her asleep. Nothing will be lost if only I do not kiss her on her lips. That I will not do. I am strong. I have resolute will."

The Fairy dropped her shimmering cloak, drew back the branches, and in another moment was hidden among them.

"I have not sinned yet," said the Prince, "nor will I." And he pushed the branches aside and saw her.

There she lay asleep already, beautiful as only the Fairy in the Garden of Paradise can be.

She smiled in her dreams; he bent over her and saw tears welling under her eyelashes.

"Do you weep for me?" he whispered. "Weep not, thou glorious woman. Only now do I understand the full bliss of Paradise; it surges through my blood, through my thoughts, through every fiber of my being. The powers of the angels, the strength of ever-

than the last. The uppermost of the portraits were so small that they seemed smaller than the tiniest rosebud when it is drawn as a point upon paper. These were millions of the Blessed, who smiled and sang, and all their songs melted together into one seemingly perfect melody.

In the middle of this hall stood a magnificent tree with handsome drooping branches; golden apples, large and small, hung like oranges from among its green leaves. This was the Tree of Knowledge of whose fruit Adam and Eve had eaten. From each leaf hung a shining red dew drop; it was as if the tree wept tears of blood.

"Let us now get into the boat," said the Fairy. "We shall find refreshment on the swelling waters. The boat rocks, but it does not leave its station; but all the lands of the earth will pass before our eyes."

And it was wonderful to behold how the whole shore moved. There came the high snow-covered Alps with their clouds and dark fir trees; the horn echoed its melancholy notes among the hills, and the shepherd yodeled sweetly in the valleys. Then banyan trees bent their long drooping branches over the boat; black swans floated on the water; and the strangest animals and flowers appeared on the shore. This was New Holland, the fifth portion of the world; it glided past them with a view of its blue hills. They heard the songs of the priests, and they saw savages dancing to the sound of skin drums and bone trumpets. Next, they saw the pyramids of Egypt, towering almost to the clouds; and fallen columns and sphinxes half-buried in sand, glided past them. Then came the northern lights shining over the extinct volcanoes near the Pole—inimitable fireworks.

The Prince saw a hundred times more than has just been described. He was happy beyond measure.

"May I stay in the Garden of Paradise always?" he asked.

"That depends upon you yourself," answered the Fairy. "If you do not, like Adam, yield to the temptation to do what is forbidden, you may always stay in the Garden of Paradise."

"I will never touch the apples on the Tree of Knowledge," said the Prince. "There are thousands of fruits here just as beautiful as those."

"Search your own heart," said the Fairy, "and if you are too weak to not do what is forbidden, then go back with the East Wind who brought you hither. He will soon be going back, and

There she lay asleep already, beautiful as only the Fairy in the
Garden of Paradise can be

will not return for a hundred years; here in the Garden of Paradise, that time will fly like a hundred hours, but even so a hundred hours is a long time for being tempted to sin.

"Every evening when I leave you, I must say 'Come with me!'
and with my hand I must beckon to you—but you must stay behind. Do not come with me. With every step you take, your longing will become greater. You will then come into the hall where
the Tree of Knowledge grows; I sleep under its fragrant drooping
boughs; you will bend over me and I must smile; but if you press
kiss upon my lips, the Garden of Paradise will sink deep into
earth and will be lost to you. Then the sharp winds of the d
wilderness will howl about you, the cold rain will drop on
head, and sorrow and labor will be your lot."

"I shall stay here," said the Prince.

The East Wind, listening, kissed the Prince on the f
and said, "Be strong, O Prince, and we shall meet here
hundred years. Farewell! Farewell!"

And the East Wind spread out his broad wings, and
like sheet-lightning in harvest time or like the north
winter.

"Farewell! Farewell!" sounded from among the fl
trees. Storks and pelicans flew away in rows like flut
and bore the East Wind company up to the bound
den of Paradise.

"Now we begin our dances," said the Fairy. "A
dance with you, when the sun goes down, you
to you; you will hear me call to you 'Come wi
obey. For a hundred years I have to repeat
every time that you resist and the trial is pas
strength. At last you will not even think
evening is the first time. Remember my wa

And the Fairy led him into a great h
lilies; the yellow stamens in each form
which sounded like violins and flutes. L
som, clad in gauzy mist, glided in the
that they would live forever, and th
would bloom forever.

At last, the sun set, and the even
light, which gave to the lilies the h
pink roses. The maidens poured o

lasting life, I feel in my mortal body. Let what will happen to me now. One moment like this is wealth enough."

And he kissed the tears from her eyes—his lips touched hers.

Then came a sound like thunder, far louder and far more awful and terrifying than any thunder that he had ever heard before; everything around him sank into the Earth. The beautiful Fairy, the flowery Garden of Paradise, sank deeper and deeper. The Prince saw it vanish like a light growing smaller and smaller in the black night; it shone far off like a tiny twinkling star. A deadly chill ran through his frame; he closed his eyes, and lay for a long time as if dead.

The cold rain fell upon his face, a keen wind roared around his head; at last his memory and his senses returned to him.

"What have I done?" he said. "I have sinned just like Adam—sinned so grievously that Paradise has again sunk beneath the earth."

He opened his eyes, and he saw the star in the distance—the star that gleamed like Paradise—it was the morning star in the sky.

He stood up, and found himself again in the great forest at the entrance to the Cavern of the Winds, and the Mother of the Winds sat by his side. She looked angry, and raised her arm in the air.

"So soon as the first evening!" she said, gesturing. "I thought as much. If you were my boy, you would go into the bag."

Then he saw Death, a strong old man, with a scythe in his hand, and great black wings, standing at the entrance to the Cavern also. "Yes, he shall go in there. Yes, he shall be laid in his coffin. But not yet; I only register him now, and then leave him for a time to wander about the earth, to expiate his sins, and to try to become a better man. But one day I shall return. When he least expects me, I shall come back and lay him in a black coffin, put it on my head, and fly up towards the star. There too the Garden of Paradise blooms. If his thoughts are good, and his heart is pious, he shall enter into it. But if his thoughts are evil and his heart still full of sin, he will sink deeper in his coffin than Paradise has sunk. I shall go only once every thousand years to see if he is to sink deeper in his coffin or to rise to the star, the twinkling star up there."

If I had been Adam, it would never have happened.

It is difficult to answer when stupid questions are asked.

What good I have done, others may tell you.

Mind you drink deeply of the spring of wisdom, and be sure to bring back a little bottleful for me.

So that is the way to the Garden of Paradise!

The eagle in the great forest flew swiftly, but the East Wind flew more swiftly still.

Such cunning pictures, only Time could record.

May I stay in the Garden of Paradise always? That depends on you yourself.

Even so, a hundred hours is a long time for being tempted to sin.

Each time that you resist and the trial is past, you will gain more strength.

The Fairy beckoned to him, and said to him, so tenderly and sweetly and charmingly, "Come with me!"

I leave him for a time to wander about the earth and to try to become a better man.

The way to Heaven is as near in the Holy Land as in England or Spain.
> —*Eleanor of Castile*, 1270

The gates of heaven are not unlocked with a golden key.
> —*Wm. Secker*, 1660

Heaven is to be at peace with things.
> —*George Santayana*, 1894

Human life is like a game of dice; if you don't get the throw you want, you must make the best of the throw you get.
> —*Terence*, 160 B.C.

Life is a game of errors; who makes the fewest wins.

—*J. H. Rhoades*, 1942

It better befits a man to laugh at life than to lament over it.

—*Seneca, c.* A.D. 60

Life is a game which has been played for untold ages, every man and woman of us being one of the two players. The chessboard is the world. . . . The rules of the game are what we call the laws of Nature. The player on the other side is hidden from us. We know that his play is always fair, just, and patient. But also we know to our cost that he never overlooks a mistake.

—*Thomas Henry Huxley*, 1870

The History of the Doasyoulikes

CHARLES KINGSLEY

"Come here, and see what happens to people who do only what is pleasant."

And the fairy, Mrs. Bedonebyasyoudid, took out of one of her cupboards (she had all sorts of mysterious cupboards in the cracks of the rocks under water) the most wonderful waterproof book, full of such photographs as never were seen. For she had found out photography (and this is a fact) more than 13,598,000 years before anybody was born; and, what is more, her photographs did not merely represent light and shade, as ours do, but colour also, and all colours, as you may see if you look at a blackcock's tail, or a butterfly's wing, or indeed most things that are or can be, so to speak. And therefore her photographs were very curious and famous, and the children, Tom and Ellie, looked with great delight for the opening of the book.

And on the title-page was written: "The History of the Great and Famous Nation of the Doasyoulikes, . . . who came away from the country of Hardwork, because they wanted to play on the harp all day long."

In the first picture, they saw these Doasyoulikes living in the land of Readymade, at the foot of the Happy-go-Lucky Mountains, where flapdoodle grows wild, and if you want to know what that is, you must read Peter Simple.

They lived very much such a life as those jolly old Greeks in Sicily, whom you may see painted on the ancient vases; and really there seemed to be great excuse for them, for they had no need to work.

Instead of houses they lived in the beautiful caves of tufa, and bathed in the warm springs three times a day; and, as for clothes, it was so warm there that the gentlemen walked about in little beside a cocked hat and a pair of straps, or some light summer tackle of that kind; and the ladies all gathered gossamer in the autumn (when they were not too lazy) to make their winter dresses.

They were very fond of music, but it was too much trouble to learn the piano or the violin; and as for dancing, that would have been too great an exertion. So they sat on anthills all day long, and played on the harp; and, if the ants bit them, why they just got up and went to the next anthill, till they were bitten there likewise.

And they sat under the flapdoodle-trees, and let the flapdoodle drop into their mouths; and under the vines, and squeezed the grape-juice down their throats; and, if any little pigs ran about ready roasted, crying "Come and eat me," as was their fashion in that country, they waited till the pigs ran against their mouths, and then took a bite, and were content, just as so many oysters would have been.

They needed no weapons, for no enemies ever came near their land; and no tools, for everything was readymade to their hand; and the stern old fairy Necessity never came near them to hunt them up, and make them use their wits, or die.

And so on, and so on, and so on, till there were never such comfortable, easy-going, happy-go-lucky people in the world.

"Well, that is a jolly life," said Tom.

"You think so?" said the fairy. "Do you see that great peaked mountain there behind," said the fairy, "with smoke coming out of its top?"

"Yes."

"And do you see all those ashes, and slag, and cinders lying about?"

"Yes."

"Then turn over the next five hundred years, and you will see what happens next."

And behold the mountain had blown up like a barrel of gunpowder, and then boiled over like a kettle; whereby one-third of the Doasyoulikes were blown into the air, and another third were smothered in ashes; so that there was only one-third left.

"You see," said the fairy, "what comes of living on a burning mountain."

"Oh, why did you not warn them?" said little Ellie.

"I did warn them all that I could. I let the smoke come out of the mountain; and wherever there is smoke there is fire. And I laid the ashes and cinders all about; and wherever there are cinders, cinders may be again. But they did not like to face facts, my dear, as very few people do; and so they invented a cock-and-bull story, which, I am sure, I never told them, that the smoke was the breath of a giant, whom some gods or other had buried under the mountain; and that the cinders were what the dwarfs roasted the little pigs whole with; and other nonsense of that kind. And, when folk are in that humor, I cannot teach them, save by the good old birch-rod."

And then she turned over the next five hundred years; and there were the remnant of the Doasyoulikes, doing as they liked, as before. They were too lazy to move away from the mountain; so they said, "If it has blown up once, that is all the more reason that it should not blow up again." And they were few in number: but they only said, "The more the merrier, but the fewer the better fare." However, that was not quite true; for all the flapdoodle-trees had been killed by the volcano, and they had eaten all the roast pigs, who, of course, could not be expected to have little ones. So they had to live very harshly, on nuts and roots which they scratched out of the ground with sticks. Some of them talked of sowing corn, as their ancestors used to do, before they came into the land of Ready-made; but they had forgotten how to make ploughs (they had forgotten even how to make harps by this time); and they had eaten all the seed-corn which they had brought out of the land of Hardwork years before; and of course it was too much trouble to go away and find more.

So they lived miserably on roots and nuts, and all the weakly little children had great stomachs, and then died.

"Why," said Tom, "they are growing no better than savages."

"And look how ugly they are all getting," said Ellie.

"Yes; and when people live on poor vegetables instead of roast beef and plum-pudding, their jaws grow large, and their lips grow coarse, like the poor people who eat only potatoes."

And she turned over the next five hundred years.

And there they were all living up in trees, and making nests to keep off the rain. And underneath the trees, lions were prowling about.

"Why," said Ellie, "the lions seem to have eaten a good many of them, for there are very few left now."

"Yes," said the fairy. "You see it was only the strongest and most active ones who could climb the trees, and so escape."

"But what great, hulking, broad-shouldered chaps they are," said Tom; "they are as rough a lot as ever I saw."

"Yes, they are getting very strong now; for the ladies will not marry any but the very strongest and fiercest gentlemen, who can help them up the trees out of the lions' way."

And she turned over the next five hundred years.

And in that time they were fewer still, and stronger, and fiercer; but their feet had changed shape very oddly, for they laid hold of the branches with their great toes, as if they had been thumbs, just as a savage may use his toes to thread his needle.

The children were very much surprised, and asked the fairy whether that was her doing.

"Yes, and no," she said, smiling. "It was only those who could use their feet as well as their hands who could get a good living; or, indeed, get married; so that they got the best of everything, and starved out all the rest; and those who are left keep up a regular breed of toe-thumb-men, as a breed of shorthorns, or skye-terriers, or fancy pigeons is kept up."

"But there is a hairy one among them," said Ellie.

"Ah!" said the fairy, "that will be a great man in his time, and chief of all the tribe."

And, when she turned over the next five hundred years, it was true.

For this hairy chief had had hairy children, and they hairier children still; and every one wished to marry hairy husbands, and have hairy children too; for the climate was growing so damp that none but the hairy ones could live: all the rest coughed and sneezed, and had sore throats, and went into consumptions, before they could grow up to be men and women.

Then the fairy turned over the next five hundred years. And they were fewer still.

"Why, there is one on the ground picking up roots," said Ellie, "and he cannot walk upright."

No more he could; for in the same way that the shape of their feet had altered, the shape of their backs had altered also.

"Why," cried Tom, "I declare they are all apes."

"Something fearfully like it, poor foolish creatures," said the fairy. "They are grown so stupid now, that they can hardly think: for none of them have used their wits for many hundred years. They have almost forgotten, too, how to talk. For each stupid child forgot some of the words it heard from its stupid parents, and had not wits enough to make fresh words for itself. Beside, they are grown so fierce and suspicious and brutal that they keep out of each other's way, and mope and sulk in the dark forests, never hearing each other's voice, till they have forgotten almost what speech is like. I am afraid they will all be apes very soon, and all by doing only what they liked."

And in the next five hundred years they were all dead and gone, by bad food and wild beasts and hunters; all except one tremendous old fellow with jaws like a jack, who stood full seven feet high; and a French explorer with a gun came up to him, and shot him, as he stood roaring and thumping his breast. And he remembered that his ancestors had once been men, and tried to say, "Am I not a man and a brother?" but had forgotten how to use his tongue; and then he tried to call for a doctor, but he had forgotten the word for one. So all he said was "Ubboboo!", and he died.

And that was the end of the great and jolly nation of the Doasyoulikes. And, when Tom and Ellie came to the end of the book, they looked very sad and solemn; and they had good reason so to do, for they really fancied that the Doasyoulikes had become apes.

"But could you not have saved them from becoming apes?" said little Ellie, at last.

"At first, my dear; if only they would have behaved like men, and set to work to do what they did not like. But the longer they waited, and behaved like the dumb beasts, who only do what they like, the stupider and clumsier they grew; till at last they were past all cure, for they had thrown their own wits away. It is such things as this that help to make me so ugly, that I know not when I shall grow fair," said Mrs. Bedonebyasyoudid.

"And where are they all now?" asked Ellie.

"Exactly where they ought to be, my dear."

"Yes!" said the fairy, solemnly, half to herself, as she closed the wonderful book. "Folk say now that I can make beasts into men, by circumstance, and selection, and competition, and so forth. Well, perhaps they are right; and perhaps, again, they are wrong. This is one of the seven things which I am forbidden to tell, till the coming of the Cocqcigrues; and, at all events, it is no concern of theirs. Whatever their ancestors were, men they are; and I advise them to behave as such, and act accordingly. But let them recollect this, that there are two sides to every question, and a downhill as well as an uphill road; and, if I can turn beasts into men, I can, by the same laws of circumstance, and selection, and competition, turn men into beasts."

They needed no weapons for no enemies ever came near their land; and no tools for everything was ready made to their hand; and the stern old fairy Necessity never came near them to hunt them up, and make them use their wits, or die.

I did warn them all I could. I let the smoke come out of the mountain, and wherever there is smoke there is fire. And I laid the ashes and the cinders all about and wherever there are cinders, cinders may be again. But they did not like to face facts, my dear, as very few people do; and so they invented a cock-and-bull story which, I am sure, I never told them.

They are grown so stupid now that they can hardly think; for none of them have used their wits for many hundred years.

There are two sides to every question, and a downhill as well as an uphill road; and if I can turn beasts into men, I can by the same laws of circumstance, and selection, and competition, turn men into beasts.

Necessity will teach a man, however stupid, to be wise.
                              —*Euripides, c. 430* B.C.
Necessity should be borne and not bemoaned.
                              —*Publilius Syrus, c. 43* B.C.
Make a virtue of necessity.
                              —*St. Jerome, c.* A.D. *400*
The hounds of Necessity snarl at his heels.
                              —*Van Wyck Mason, 1940*
A wise man will see to it that his acts always seem voluntary and
    not done by compulsion, however much he may be compelled
    by necessity.
                              —*Machiavelli* (1469–1527)

The Locksmith and the Stranger

EDMUND C. BERKELEY

Once there was a man who was in the business of making locks
and keys and who was very skillful. One day a stranger walked into
his shop and said to him, "I want you to make a key which will
open a certain safe." The locksmith said to him, "Whose safe is it?"
The stranger said, "Never you mind whose safe it is. I will pay you
handsomely for the key. I'll blindfold you and take you to the
place where the safe is. You can have all the tools you want—I'll
pay for them—and you make me a key. Besides, while you make
the key, you will have a chance to work out some intensely interesting scientific theories, and after the safe is cracked open, I will
give you permission to publish some papers, those that don't reveal
too much information. Think it over; I'll be back tomorrow."

So the locksmith wondered about the remark "Never you mind"

and the blindfolding and the secrecy; but he knew it was hard enough to earn a living, and the promise of the stranger sounded attractive and exciting. So he said to himself, "Well, that fellow would just get another locksmith if I did not go," and so he decided that he would go. And the next morning the stranger came for him, and he allowed himself to be blindfolded and he went.

For several years the locksmith tried to open the safe, and then at last he succeeded. But the stranger did not allow him to look inside; all the locksmith saw was the door swing open. The stranger said to him, "Here is your pay—now go away—and remember not to talk about this, or you will get into a lot of trouble."

After a few more weeks, the locksmith read in the newspaper that what the stranger had taken out of the safe was a supremely intelligent directing mechanism for flying weapons. They ranged from the size of a wasp to the size of an eagle, and they would enable him to pinpoint and exterminate any person, any community, any town, any city in the whole world. And he read the stranger's declaration that henceforth the world was to do exactly as he commanded, and that any opposition to his commands would be precisely and completely destroyed.

No healing can be found for evil once wrought.
                              —*Homer, c.* 850 B.C.
The evil that lies concealed is always the most serious.
                              —*Publilius Syrus, c.* 43 B.C.
Every evil in the bud is easily crushed.
                              —*Cicero,* 43 B.C.
It is not comforting to know that your skills and your work have forged a link in a chain of evil.

The Elephant and the Donkey

JAMES RESTON

Once upon a time there was a big elephant who ruled over the animal kingdom for four long years, surveying the universe from his big flying machine, appearing occasionally on television and preaching the gospel of peace, prosperity, law and order.

Now this was a pretty restless time. The other big elephants were doing all right and the fat cats were dining on cream and honey. Everything looked fairly good, particularly the cute chicks who had long hair and very short skirts, but a lot of the little animals were in trouble, and some of them were even hungry.

So one day a little donkey from the prairies came along and said he thought the animal kingdom needed a new leader, for example, himself; and the No. 1 elephant just laughed.

"Look at the facts," the donkey said. "The elephant talks of peace, but there is no peace. He talks of prosperity, but over five million animals are out of work. He boasts about good times but the mice are paying 20 per cent more for cheese. He promised to bring the lions and the lambs together, but the lions ate up all the lambs and even the tigers are scared to go out in the forest after dark."

"Listen to the jackass," said the elephant. "I won't reply to this rubbish, but I will say this: Who made peace with the bear? Who flew to the very middle of the animal kingdom and tamed the dragon? Who saved half a million grunts from the great swamp where they were sinking when I took over the kingdom?"

At this all the elephants began waving their trunks and shouting, "Four More Years," and the jackals joined in and began barking at the donkeys.

"I have been misrepresented by the monkeys," the No. 1 elephant continued. "They go around chattering against me in the night. They call me names, and I have big ears. They publish their slanders on every tree in the forest, and the elephant remembers."

"Eight More Years," roared the bears, who were lolling at the edge of the forest gobbling cheap wheat. "Twelve More Years," insisted the fat cats.

The elephant threw his trunk over one tusk, wiped the TV make-up off his face and grinned. "I don't say everything is perfect in the animal kingdom. There has been some loose living around here. I have seen the long-haired dogs in the poppy patch. I have seen the roosters chasing the chicks, and even vice versa. And there is crime and profiteering and unemployment.

"But these are not the important things. All animals must learn to see things as the elephant sees them: from on high. If you are hungry, you must realize that most animals are not hungry. If you are old or sick you must understand that most animals are not old and sick. It is the generality of things that counts. The lions may be eating the lambs, but the rate of lamb-eating has gone down two-tenths of one per cent in the last four years, and who can match that?" (Cries of "Sixteen More Years.")

"I can," brayed the donkey and demanded equal time. "The elephant remembers what he wants to remember," the donkey said. "A hungry doe can't eat the gross animal product. A lamb in the claws of a lion can't concentrate on the declining rate of the lion's appetite. It has to think about the decline of lambs.

"Any jackass knows that. The elephant says he made peace with the bear and tamed the dragon and rescued the grunts, but the bear took our grain and is still helping to kill the grunts. He didn't tame them, he bribed them, and what did the mice around here get out of all that?

"The elephant is deceiving you. He covers up his blunders. He works with the bugs to spy on the donkeys in the night. He makes deals with the bears at our expense. The survival of the fittest in our kingdom has been replaced by the triumph of the trickiest. What this forest needs is a good honest clumsy jackass."

But the snakes hissed and the bears growled and the lions roared and the fat cats merely grinned, and most of the animals cheered the elephant, and their cries shook the forest. "Twenty More Years," they shouted. "Make it forty," roared the jackals, and the elephant smiled and winked at the fat cats.

Moral: Truth is indeed much stranger than fiction.

The fat cats were dining on cream and honey.
The elephant talks of peace but there is no peace.
All animals must learn to see things as the elephant sees them.
The survival of the fittest in our kingdom has been replaced by the
   triumph of the trickiest.

Where That Superhighway Runs, There Used to Be a Cornfield

ROBERT REDFIELD

One day as I sat on an old bench near my house on the outskirts
of Chicago, a stranger appeared and sat down beside me.

"Do you mind if I join you?" he asked. "There is some information I want very much to get. But perhaps I interrupt your
thoughts?"

I told him that my thoughts were at the moment not much—I
had been trying to think of an address I was to give to some college
students.

He asked me what I would say to them.

"Give them good advice," I replied. "That is the usual thing
to do."

"About what?" He seemed really interested.

"I don't quite know," was my answer, "but the usual thing is to
tell them about the importance of the free mind and the privilege
they enjoy in getting an education. And that sort of thing. You
know—exhort them and commend them and encourage them."

"If you can advise them," said the stranger, "perhaps you can
advise me."

I remembered that he had said he wanted information. My first thought had been that he would ask me about what kind of dog-food I bought for my dog—you know, market research—or that perhaps he was making a political canvass of our neighborhood. But his first question showed me that these guesses were very wrong.

"I wish you would explain to me about this war that I hear is going on—the war that is now cold and might get hot. Are you people at war with each other?"

That didn't seem to me the way to put it. I started to explain. "The Russians want to conquer everybody, by propaganda if they can and by force if they have to. So they make monstrous weapons that threaten us, and that force us to make monstrous weapons to threaten them. We have some bombs big enough to kill millions of people that we carry around in airplanes in case the Russians begin to drop bombs on us. For the Russians have bombs just as big, and now they are learning how to shoot them over to us with rockets or maybe pretty soon from space-ships circling overhead. So of course there is a kind of war—two sides all ready to shoot at each other."

He didn't say anything for a while. He seemed to be thinking. Then he said, "Tell me, do you yourself know anything about war?"

"Well, yes." I tried to sound modest. "I had some personal connection with a war in 1917 and I saw something of another one in the 1940's."

"And this cold war you speak of," he continued, "when it becomes hot, when the monster bombs are dropped, will it be like those old wars you knew?"

At once I understood that it would be quite different. But I found it hard to get out the words that would describe the new thing we were calling war. I thought of the sober estimates of scientific advisors to our President that if the bombs are set off, whether by design or by accident, about sixty million Americans would be killed, our greater cities would be reduced to ruin, and the survivors—in whatever appalling chaos they might find themselves—as well as their children and children's children would be poisoned and distorted to an extent impossible to predict. I thought of this and knew that the provincial little massacre I witnessed on the Aisne River in 1917 was something else again. I thought, but I could say little.

"No, it would be a new kind of experience," I said.

"Then," said the stranger, "it should have a different name. Not 'war.' 'Mutual suicide,' perhaps. Or maybe I should put it down that you people are getting ready for your own partial extermination. Is that it?"

I felt I was becoming confused. And a little annoyed with my visitor. I didn't like the way he kept saying "you people." What did he mean by "you people"? I asked him that in so many words.

"Oh," he said, "you people—you, and Khrushchev and the young college people you are going to talk to and John Foster Dulles and the boys down at the corner in Brooklyn and those fishermen drawing up their nets on the Malabar coast."

He did talk in a strange way. Where had he come from? I tried to get our conversation back into easier paths.

"Do *you* come from India?" I asked.

"No," he said, "no. I come from farther away than that."

He sat silent and I tried to get a good look at him. But although he sat close to me on the bench, I could not see him well because the sun was setting just behind him. It was he who took up the conversation. "I suppose you people want to go on living?"

I said that most of us did.

"Then," he said, "I suppose you people are doing what you can to prevent this thing that you call a war but would not be a war but a kind of suicide?"

"We are doing what we can," I replied. "In this country we are spending more money for missiles and maybe we can get the Europeans to put our missiles on their land nearer to the Russians and maybe we can build space-ships before the Russians do and so get the drop on them that way. We have been working pretty hard to make our weapons as big as or bigger than the Russians' weapons. You know we were the first to kill people with atomic bombs and we were the first to make bombs one thousand times bigger than the little ones that killed only about seventy-five thousand people apiece in Japan. We had to make the very big bombs because if we hadn't the Russians would have made them first and then we wouldn't have had security. Neither side wants to start a war when it is clear that the starter would be destroyed also. Of course it is true that the Russians made the very big bombs too and now they are going after space and the moon and we have to go after these things too. Two-thirds of the national budget for next year will be used for military purposes of one kind or another. So we *are* trying to prevent it from happening."

He made a gesture of interruption. "You go too fast," he said. "I can't quite follow. You say you Americans are doing these things for security? And you Russians are doing these things too?"

You Russians! He addressed *me* as "you Russians"! I took him up. "I can't speak for the Russians," I said. "We can't trust the Russians."

"Why not?" he asked. "Don't they want to live too? And can't you trust their common interest with you in continuing to live? It seems to me quite a basis for getting together on some arrangement not to shoot at each other. Two men with firebrands in a room of explosives share one very immediate common interest. But there is something else in what you just said that puzzles me. I think you told me that you went ahead with making more monstrous weapons in order to have security. Tell me, now that you have the thousand-times-bigger bombs, do you feel more secure?"

My impatience had subsided, and, besides, I saw that he had a point or two. I tried to answer his question honestly.

"No," I said, "I don't really feel more secure now than before we had the hydrogen bomb. For at least two reasons. The destruction that could be done now is very much greater—all civilization could be blown to bits. And also, so many countries are getting the weapons and their management is getting so difficult and complicated that the decisions whether or not to fire a missile or drop a bomb must be left to many different people—base commanders, airplane pilots and so on—so that the chance that the first big explosion might occur through a misunderstanding or a rash act grows greater and greater. We might more and more easily have a catastrophe by a sort of inevitable accident. No, I don't feel more secure."

He was thoughtful. Then he spoke again.

"I shouldn't express an opinion. But I can say I am confused. You seem to be telling me that you are working hard to prevent this mutual suicide by making bigger and bigger weapons to shoot at each other, and that the more you make, the more likely they will go off of themselves. It is like piling more and more explosives into this room with the two waving firebrands. It seems a strange way to seek security."

Again there was a silence. Then he asked me if I thought that the young college people would continue to choose the same way to security when they took over matters. I told him that I could not predict as to that.

"They might find some other way," he said. "They might call the thing that you are trying to prevent not war but mutual destruction. They might become less bellicose about that struggle that is now going on between some of you and others of you. They might talk less about how each wants to destroy the other and fears to be destroyed by the other and talk more with each other about your common interests—in keeping alive, in keeping down the cost of threatening each other. They might even move some of the explosives out of the room—what difference would that make to mutual security if each can destroy the other several times over with the explosives that are left? They might even stamp out the firebrands and walk away from the explosives.

"These young people don't *have* to do just what you have been doing," he continued. "They will do better. They are more experienced than you."

"*Less* experienced, I think you mean," said I.

"No, I mean more experienced. They start knowing not only what you know but also what you did—which is more than you knew when you started. So they are a more experienced people than you. And I suppose I am at liberty to believe that you people learn by experience? That you do things better as you go along?"

"Yes," said I. "That is progress. Progress is something we all believe in. Or maybe used to believe in. There seem to be doubts now about progress. Progress, it appears, is not going forward step by step, or leap by leap, to the better and better. It seems to me like going ahead and backward at one and the same time, by the same effort of movement. Or like—"

"Like what?" he asked.

"Like a strange dream in which one opens door after door down a corridor with a light at the end of it only to find that each door opened makes the light brighter and the darkness darker. There is more light all the time: the antibiotics and the good music that comes out of my loudspeaker and the old slums torn down. And there is also more darkness: people living longer to suffer from other diseases, and many wasted hours in front of the TV, and the new slums growing up around the overcrowded cities. Progress seems to me very untrustworthy. She can't just be believed in. She has somehow to be managed."

"You are becoming eloquent," he said. "If I may say so without offense, eloquence is like progress—bright and shining, but untrustworthy. Let us try again to understand the problem of how to go forward without going backward, to let new light shine undarkened. May I ask how you people are doing with space control?"

"Not much—yet," I said. "We have put some satellites into orbit and our President proposed that space be controlled internationally—an interplanetary police force, some day—"

He interrupted. "You misunderstand me. I referred not to interplanetary space—which by the way seems to me a very poor place to be—but to space right here, on your own planet, where you people live. How are you people doing with respect to control of your own terrestrial space?"

I remembered a piece I had been reading about how badly we had been doing, and I recalled some facts about occupation of terrestrial space. So I began at once to provide the stranger with information about the topic he had just raised.

"The population of our planet is increasing at a rate of about 40,000,000 a year. By 1987, when college students of today are putting their children through college, at the present rate of growth there will be about six and a half billion people. The world will then be more than twice as crowded as it is now. China will have a population of five billion people in a hundred years if the present rate of growth continues. Indeed, stranger, if your wish was to get to know us, you have come at a favorable time, for about twenty per cent of all the people who ever lived are alive now. But more important than this great number of us is the fact that the rate of increase overcomes much of the advantages we think we give ourselves by modern medicine and technology. The Egyptians are probably poorer than ever because there are so many more of them. Most of the increase that India has achieved by better technology and planning is no real increase at all because medicine and hygiene have caused the number of people who eat the food to increase as rapidly as the food has."

"You do indeed go forward backward toward a darkened light," said he. "However," he continued, "you don't look so badly off right around here—on this American patch of your terrestrial space."

"We are very proud, we Americans, of our standard of living. I will give you another statistic. It is estimated that with present technology this planet of ours could support, with the standard of living enjoyed by Americans, less than one-third of the people who are now on it. So some of us are doing pretty well. And we shall probably do better.

"On this earth the rich nations are getting richer. Of course the poor ones are getting poorer."

"That does not sound like a very desirable arrangement," the stranger went on. "It must cause some hard feelings. And I suppose you people who are Americans do pretty well by making and consuming things? Don't you ever use up any of the things you need for getting along better?"

I had still another statistic for him. "The people of my nation, with about seven per cent of the world's population, are now absorbing about sixty per cent of the world's minerals—mostly irreplaceable. We are indeed great consumers. We consume raw materials, use up water so it sometimes has to be rationed in cities, pollute air and rivers with waste products, and almost take pride in the piles of junked automobiles. It all goes to make the American standard of living the highest on earth. Now that I understand that it is the control of terrestrial space in which you are interested, I can say that we overrun it rather than control it."

He was silent and thoughtful. "What is that great wall of earth over there?" he suddenly asked. I followed the line of his gaze.

"That is a superhighway under construction. It will get more people around places faster."

"It certainly overruns space," he remarked. This time I did not say what was on my mind—that industry and highways take out of agricultural use about a million acres of American land yearly, and the prediction that the agricultural surpluses that are now so troublesome will be only a memory twenty years from now. Instead

I said that Chicago was growing very fast and needed better transportation.

"You are indeed an odd people," he said. "In your efforts to get security from war you make yourselves more and more insecure; in your efforts to get a good life, you rather mess up much of the life you are busy improving. This is indeed a darkened light."

The sun had set now and the twilight made that wall of earth loom larger against the amber sky. My mind, perhaps tired by the effort to explain how things are on this earth, relaxed into reminiscence, into dreamy consideration of times past. I said something like this to the stranger.

"Where that superhighway runs, there used to be a cornfield. In June the unfolding leaves made a neat, fresh carpet there—nine acres of it. In August one walked slowly between the rows of stalks, taller than one's head. When we went into the corn on very hot nights and stood still and listened, we used to tell ourselves that we heard the corn growing. And over there farther, there was a piece of aboriginal prairie that had never been broken by the plow. Only native plants grew there, prairie dock and tickseed, downy phlox and bluegrass. And up there where there are so many houses, the oaks stood very old and tall, and I used to find yellow adder's tongue growing beneath some of them.

"Do you know what I miss? I am thinking just now, although the season of the year is not appropriate, that I miss very much the sound of the whetstone on the scythe—a good, clean sound. Oh, and many other things I miss—the voice of the bobwhite, the flight of the redheaded woodpecker as he flashed along the dirt road to fling himself like a painted dart against a telephone pole. And I miss the fields filled with shooting stars. And the clang and rattle of the windmill when the vanes swung around in a shift of breeze, and the puddles of water at the well where the wasps came in summer.

"Excuse me," I said. "This must bore you. Older people tend to look back on things that are gone and were good to them. If now you were talking to a young person, he would not have on his mind these changes that are losses to me. It is a great and necessary thing about young people that they look forward with a confidence unshaken by such regrets. It is a good thing that some things are unremembered as the generations pass. Really you should be talking to the young people. Why don't you go to some college town and talk to young people?"

He told me that he might do just that. I could see that indeed he was growing tired of me. Neither of us spoke for a time and in the growing dusk I thought I could see him looking through the pages of a notebook.

"Young people," he said. "I do have some notes on the topic. I have been looking into some of the authorities you have on young people, at least young people who are Americans. I have here a summary of the results of research on this subject. Yes, here it is: 'American young people are uncommitted and other-directed; they have no heroes and few illusions; they seek security and togetherness; they want only to find places in the slots of employment and safe advancement; after comfortable years in college they become organization men and succumb slowly to creeping contentment.'"

His words stirred me to a disagreement, even resentment, that I could not at once express. Was this true of our young people? I wanted to argue the matter with him but could not find the words. But my resentment was growing. Somehow I felt that the view of us people that he was developing was incomplete. He saw us, but in a queer, unnatural light, a light from firebrands and neon signs. It was true, and yet it was not true. Or not all the truth, and my resentment was directed also at myself, for had I not been telling him things, true things yet not all the truth, about us. Somehow I had responded to him in such a way as to help him to form this true yet not quite true view of us. I wanted to turn upon him, to make *him* say something, make some observations that I could contradict. He had risen and I saw he was about to leave me.

"Stranger," I said, "before you go won't you tell me what your impressions are, on the whole, thinking over what you know about us, all of us here?"

When he did speak his words were only one more question. "How do *you* know all these things you have been telling me, about war and space control and the multiplication of people and so on?"

"I read things," I said, "and then we have many studies of these

matters. And commissions and reports and committees and conferences."

"I see," he said. "You have commissions and reports and conferences. Tell me, did you ever have a conference on the good
life?"

"On what?"

"On the good life. On what a good life would be for all you
people. Just in case you stamp out the firebrands and go on living
with yourselves. A conference as to what would be a good life, for
everybody, given the limitations of earth and space and the nature,
whatever it is, of all of you."

"It seems a large subject. And not too definite. How would such
a conference be organized?"

"I think I could make some suggestions," said the stranger. "I
could propose a tentative agenda. The topics could be formulated
for group discussion in the form of a list of questions. Like this:

ITEM ONE: Do you want more and more people existing together
somehow or do you want not quite so many people living well?

ITEM TWO: What is growth—is it getting bigger or getting better?

ITEM THREE: What is a good standard of living, more things to
consume or better things to appreciate and discriminate? This
third item on the agenda would require much subdivision and consideration of particular subtopics. You could appoint a subcommit-
tee for each subtopic, you know. For example, Subtopic 37,
Production and Consumption, Subsubtopic 49, division b, 3: Do
you want to buy the car of tomorrow today only to find that tomorrow it is already the car of yesterday and you are expected to
buy another? And so on. Oh, it could be quite an agenda.

ITEM FOUR: What is the right relation of man to the cosmos?
Again, a subtopic: Which is the better use of the moon: to hit it
with a rocket or just to look at it?

ITEM FIVE: Where are the frontiers of human enterprise? That
item could be put in different ways, for example: Should people
build and pioneer always outward or sometimes inward?

He must have seen that I still looked puzzled. So he tried again.
"Item Five could be put more concretely," he said. "Like this: To
take risks, make adventures, create and add to human life, is it

necessary to climb a mountain or build a space-ship, or could one also adventure and create within a limited world? Find new good things within the limits of earth-space, production and consumption? Exercise restraints to free one's self for the making of new things for enjoyment, improved experience, wiser and finer judgments? Where is freedom? In always doing more and more or in doing fewer things to do them better? That, of course, amounts to asking if the very abundance of material goods may not result in a loss of freedom."

I was trying to take this in. "It would certainly be a difficult conference to organize," I said. "And it would make some people very uneasy. It seems to ask questions that are somehow, where I live, not quite the sort of question to ask. And so different from what is discussed at the conferences that I do go to! Those conferences are concerned with how to do things. Your conference would be concerned with why one should do them at all. And with what is good to do and why."

"Just so," he said. "And now I say goodbye. It has been nice knowing you people. You *are* odd, and, from what I have seen of you, pretty mixed up. But I wish you well. Goodbye."

He was gone, and I have not seen him since. But what he said is much in my mind.

"Maybe I should put it down that you people are getting ready for your own partial extermination. Is that it?"

"Tell me, now that you have the thousand-times bigger bombs, do you feel more secure?"—"No," I said. "I don't really feel more secure now than before we had the hydrogen bomb."

The management of the weapons is getting so difficult and complicated that the decisions whether or not to fire a missile or drop a bomb must be left to many different people—so that the chance that the first big explosion might occur through a misunderstanding or a rash act grow greater and greater. We

might more and more easily have a catastrophe by a sort of inevitable accident.

Two men with firebrands in a room of explosives share one very
immediate common interest.

Progress, it appears, is not step by step or leap by leap to the better
and better—but like going ahead and backward at one and the
same time.

Progress is like a strange dream in which one opens door after door
down a corridor with a light at the end of it, only to find that
each door opened makes the light brighter and the darkness
darker.

"You do indeed go forward backward toward a darkened light."

"You are indeed an odd people," he said. "In your efforts to get
security from war, you make yourselves more and more insecure; in your efforts to get a good life, you rather mess up
much of the life you are busy improving. This is indeed a
darkened light."

What is growth—is it getting bigger or getting better?

Which is the better use of the moon: to hit it with a rocket or
just to look at it?

The Fire Squirrels

EDMUND C. BERKELEY

Scene: Two squirrels, a young one named Quo, and an older one
named Cra-Cra, are sitting by a small campfire in a field at the
edge of a wood. Behind them, hung on a low branch of a tree, are
two squirrel-size hammocks. Over each of the hammocks is a small
canopy that can be lowered to keep out biting insects. It is a pleasant summer evening; the sun has just recently set, and the stars
are coming out.

Quo: Cra-Cra, you know I don't believe the old myths any more.
Tell me again how it really happened.

Cra-Cra: Just this: we received our chance because they dropped theirs. It is as simple as that.

Quo: In other words, they were the first animals to use tools, and we are the second?

Cra-Cra: Yes. There is a mode of surviving in the world of nature which depends on using tools and having know-how. Language is an important part of that mode, so that individuals can talk to each other, share knowledge about tools, and pass that knowledge on from one generation to the next. Just copycatting, just imitation, which a great many animals use, is very limited; language gets around those limits. And a powerful early tool is fire. The mastery of fire is an excellent test for animals that aspire to tool-using—it tests curiosity, observation, perseverance, intelligence, common sense, and probably some more attributes. The tool-using mode of surviving is called the cultural corridor.

Quo: I see. (*He picks up a stick, and puts it on the fire to burn.*)

Cra-Cra: They were the first animals to use fire and to occupy the cultural corridor. But they dropped their chance. They failed to qualify for permanent occupancy.

Quo: Why?

Cra-Cra: In a way, you could have predicted that they would fail. In evolution, the first creature to occupy a corridor, a niche in the world of nature, is often a misfit. It regularly drops the chance. This was true, for example, of the pterodactyls, the first reptiles who developed wings and flew through the air like birds. In the airways of the planet, the pterodactyls preceded the birds, and are extinct.

Quo: How did the first species in the cultural corridor drop their chance?

Cra-Cra: They killed themselves off. That's perfectly clear from the fossil record, and from such of their written records as we have deciphered. Also, the main reason is clear: they had a severely limited set of emotions; for that set of emotions, they learned too much about the forces of nature and how to release those forces. A case of mismatch.

It is clear that they devoted most of their knowledge to destruction of each other. Their social inventions as a species included fighting and killing among themselves, war. But we squirrels have never invented fighting and killing among ourselves. It is contrary to our nature. Of course, we have disputes and even hatred and some oppression. To deal with these, we use bluff and gestures, as all animals do; also we use voting to see which side is more numerous, as many herd animals do; but we always work out an accommodation, an arrangement, that is rather fair and reasonable.

Quo: Yes, I know that. But how were we able to occupy the cultural corridor? (*He puts another stick on the fire to burn.*)

Cra-Cra: Since we are not warlike, we never contested their occupation of the cultural corridor. But after they died off, became extinct like the dinosaurs, the corridor was empty again. We were watching and we were waiting. When they were gone, we evolved quickly, because of our quick generations, for something like thirty thousand years; and we mastered tools and fire and language, and we entered the cultural corridor.

I have heard our authorities say that if squirrels had been any bigger than they had been in those earlier years, the squirrels too would almost surely have been killed off, literally—or enslaved, literally, like what they called "domesticated animals," who were completely dependent on masters, no longer able to survive without masters.

But we are small—we have to be in order to run through the trees—and in those days we were smaller still. We were independent—what they called "wild animals." And we are rodents, like the rats and the mice and the beavers; and we have a very strong grip on life. Quo, you can be proud you are a rodent.

Quo: What did they call themselves?

Cra-Cra: According to the records that we have deciphered, they called themselves *homo sapiens,* which literally translated would be "the wise man." But they ought to have called themselves *homo brutus,* "the beast man." And we squirrels call them the fire apes.

The mastery of fire is an excellent test for animals that aspire to tool-using; it tests curiosity, observation, perseverance, intelligence, common sense, and probably some more attributes.

The first creature to occupy a corridor, a niche, in the world of nature is often a misfit.

They had a severely limited set of emotions; for that set of emotions they learned too much about the forces of nature and how to release those forces: a case of mismatch.

We always work out an accommodation, an arrangement, that is on the whole rather fair and reasonable.

They called themselves *homo sapiens,* which literally translated would be "the wise man." But they ought to have called themselves *homo brutus,* "the beast man." And we squirrels call them the fire apes.

The advantage of the emotions is that they lead us astray.
—*Oscar Wilde, 1891*

For a hundred million years those little mammals waited. . . . no one would have imagined that the gray and infinitely complex convolutions of the human brain were locked away in the forebrain of an insectivorous creature no larger than a rat. An observer waiting for some sign of creative emergence among those little animals in the underbrush would have grown weary as years by the million flowed away. He would have sworn that every variation in the game of life had been exploited and played out—that the reptiles were the master form —that the mammals were effective only upon an infinitely small size level.
—*Loren C. Eiseley, 1949*

A child plays with fire but a mature man understands it, controls it, and uses it.

Oh, that we could see ourselves as others see us.

Without vision the people perish.

Thoughtless technology is a curse.

Part II

ON
FLATTERY
AND
PERSUASION

THE · FOX AND THE · CROW.

The Crow and the Fox

JEAN DE LA FONTAINE

Master Crow, perched high in a tree, held in his beak a large piece of excellent cheese.

Master Fox, drawn thither by the appetizing smell, called up to him and said:

"Oh, good morning, Lord Crow! How handsome you are! How beautiful you are! To tell the truth, if your voice is like your feathers, you are the king, the phoenix, of all the animals in these woods."

At these words, the Crow was overwhelmed with joy. And, to show off his beautiful voice, he opened his great beak and called, "Caw, caw, caw," but he dropped his prize.

The Fox seized it at once, and said, over his shoulder as he departed:

"My good fellow, know that every flatterer lives at the expense of those who listen to him. Certainly that lesson is well worth a whole cheese."

The Crow, ashamed and humiliated, swore an oath—but a little late—that never again would he be so tricked.

A flattering speech is honeyed poison.
—*Publilius Syrus, c. 43* B.C.

A man that flattereth his neighbor spreadeth a net for his feet.
—*John Bunyan, 1678*

Among all the pestilences that there be in friendships, the greatest is flattery.
—*Geoffrey Chaucer* (1340?–1400)

Flattery is like Cologne water, to be smelt of, not swallowed.
—*Josh Billings, 1858*

The Visitor Who Got a Lot
for Three Dollars

GEORGE ADE

The Learned Phrenologist sat in his office surrounded by his whiskers.

Now and then he put a forefinger to his brow and glanced at the mirror to make sure that he still resembled William Cullen Bryant.

Near him, on a table, was a pallid head made of plaster-of-paris and stickily ornamented with small labels. On the wall was a chart showing that the orangutan does not have Daniel Webster's facial angle.

"Is the graft played out?" asked the Learned Phrenologist, as he waited. "Is science up against it or what?"

Then he heard the fall of heavy feet and resumed his imitation. The door opened and there came into the room a tall, rangy person with a head in the shape of a Rocky Ford cantaloupe.

Aroused from his meditation, the Learned Phrenologist looked up at the stranger as through a glass, darkly, and pointed to a red plush chair.

The Easy Mark collapsed into the boarding-house chair and the man with more whiskers than Darwin ever saw stood behind him and ran his fingers over his head, tarantula-wise.

"Well, well!" said the Learned Phrenologist. "Enough benevolence here to do a family of eight. Courage? I guess yes! Dewey's got the same kind of a lump right over the left ear. Love of home and friends—like the ridge behind a bunker! Firmness—out of sight! Reverence—well, when it comes to reverence, you're certainly there with the goods! Conscientiousness, hopes and ideality —the limit! And as for metaphysical penetration—oh, say, the metaphysical penetration, right where you part the hair—oh, Laura! Say, you've got Charles Eliot Norton whipped to a custard. I've got my hand on it now. You can feel it yourself, can't you?"

"I can feel something," replied the Easy Mark, with a rapt smile.

"Wit, compassion and poetic talent—right here where I've got my thumb—I think you'll run as high as 98 per cent on all the intellectual faculties. In your case we have a rare combination of executive ability, or the power to command, and those qualities of benevolence and ideality which contribute to the fostering of permanent religious sentiment. I don't know what your present occupation is, but you ought to be president of a theological seminary. Kindly slip me three dollars before you pass out."

The tall man separated himself from two days' pay and then went out on the street and pushed people off the sidewalk, he thought so well of himself.

Thereafter, as before, he drove a truck, but he was always glad to know that he could have been president of a theological seminary.

Moral: A good jolly is worth whatever you pay for it.

Flattery, formerly a vice, is now a fashion.
                    —*Publilius Syrus, c.* 43 B.C.
'Tis an old maxim in the schools
That flattery's the food of fools:
Yet now and then your men of wit
Will condescend to take a bit.

                    —*Jonathan Swift,* 1713
We sometimes think that we hate flattery, but we hate only the
    manner in which it is done.

                    —*La Rochefoucauld,* 1665
What valor cannot win, flattery may.

                    —*Publilius Syrus, c.* 43 B.C.
If you flatter everyone, who will be your enemy?

                    —*Chinese proverb*
Everyone likes flattery; and when you come to Royalty, you should
    lay it on with a trowel.

                    —*Benjamin Disraeli* (1804–1884)

The Cuckoo and the Eagle

IVAN A. KRYLOV

The Eagle directed that the Cuckoo be promoted to the rank of Nightingale.

The Cuckoo, proud of his new position, perched on an aspen and started singing for all he was worth.

After a time, he looked around. All the birds were flying here and there, some laughing at him, others calling him names. The Cuckoo became angry and hastened back to the Eagle, complaining of his reception among the birds.

"Help me, Sire," he said. "By your command I have been promoted to the position of Nightingale to these woods. But the birds laugh and scoff at my song."

"My friend," said the Eagle, "I am a king, but not God. I can direct that a Cuckoo be ranked as a Nightingale, but I cannot *make* a Nightingale out of a Cuckoo."

What really flatters a man is that you think him worth flattering.
 —*George Bernard Shaw, 1904*
A fool who is flattered becomes even more of a fool.

The Wind and the Sun

AESOP

The Wind and the Sun argued as to which was the stronger. They agreed that the test should be who could first strip a Traveler of his cloak.

THE·LION·IN·LOVE·

The Wind first tried his strength and blew with all his might; but the keener the blasts, the closer the Traveler wrapped himself up in his cloak. At last, losing hope of winning the argument, the Wind challenged the Sun to try what he could accomplish.

The Sun at once started shining with utmost warmth. The Traveler soon felt the sunny rays, started mopping his brow, and then took off his cloak and jacket also.

Moral: Persuasion accomplishes more than force.

Win by persuasion, not force.

—*Latin proverb*

The pen is mightier than the sword.

—*Lord Lytton, 1838*

Persuasion accomplishes more than force.

The Lion in Love

AESOP

Once there was a Lion who fell deeply in love with a charming maiden, who was a Woodcutter's daughter. And he asked the Woodcutter for her hand in marriage.

The Woodcutter was not pleased with the prospect of so dangerous a member of the family. Respectfully and timidly he declined. But the King of the Beasts roared with anger, and threatened him with harm.

So the Woodcutter took thought, and said, "Your Royal Highness, my daughter and I are greatly honored by your noble proposal. But you have such great sharp teeth and such long sharp claws that my daughter is very much frightened of them. If you

THE·CROW AND THE·MUSSEL·

have your teeth pulled, and your claws removed, then we can consider you as a bridegroom for my daughter."

The Lion thought about this and hesitated. But being very much in love, he sought out a Surgeon and submitted to the removal of his teeth and claws. He then returned to the Woodcutter without teeth and claws, to press his suit and claim the maiden.

But the Woodcutter, no longer afraid of the Lion, seized a stout club, beat the Lion, and drove him away.

An extravagant love consults neither life, fortune, nor reputation, but sacrifices all that can be dear to a man of sense and honour, to the transports of an inconsiderate passion.
—*Sir Roger L'Estrange*
There is danger in being persuaded before one understands.
—*Thomas Wilson, 1755*

The Crow and the Mussel

AESOP AND E.C.B.

Once a young crow came upon a mussel. Its two shells were tight shut, and it was heavy, showing that the mussel was still inside.

Taking the mussel in his beak, he tried to crack the shell by dashing it against a rock. But the shell was too strong.

An old crow nearby came up to the young crow and said, "May I give you a suggestion? I don't believe that you can break it that way. If you take it high in the air, and drop it on a rock, then it will break and you can get at the mussel."

The young crow thought that sounded like a fine idea. Saying "Thanks" to the old crow, he flew high in the air, aimed, dropped the mussel square on the rock, and saw it break.

But the old crow waiting near the rock quickly snapped up the mussel, laughed at the young crow arriving in haste, and flew away.

The young crow said to himself, "Well, it is a good method—even if this time I had to pay for learning it."

Timeo Danaos, et dona ferentes. Two translations of the Latin:
    I fear the Greeks, even bearing gifts.
    I fear the Greeks, and the gifts they bear.
                               —Vergil, 19 B.C.
Charity begins at home, they say; and most people are kind to their neighbours for their own sakes.
                         —Sir Roger L'Estrange
Beware of persuasion from interested parties.
Never decide to buy something while listening to the salesman.

The Two Raccoons and the Button

EDMUND C. BERKELEY

George Raccoon: Oh, darn, there's a button off my shirt.

Martha Raccoon: My dear, see if there isn't another shirt in your drawer that you can wear.

George: (searching) No, there isn't. That's the only clean white shirt; all the others are gray. And I have to wear a white shirt to-day; there's a meeting this morning with Mr. Wolf and Mr. Fox—we have a problem with the Bears, you know.

Martha: I'm sure there is another white shirt. (She comes and searches the drawer.) Well, there isn't one, you're right. Do you have the button?

George: Yes, here it is. Oh, Martha, are you going to sew it on for me right now? You're amazing, you're wonderful!

Martha: Give me the button. (She swiftly sews the button on the white shirt, while he waits patiently.) There's your shirt.

George: Oh, thank you—you're my dear Martha. You're the best and nicest help a Raccoon could ask for. I just don't know what I'd do without you.

Martha: (smiling) I know what you'd do, you big Raccoon— you'd sew it on yourself, just as you used to before you married me—and you'd save all that flattery.

George: (giving her a Raccoon hug) Not flattery, my dear— persuasion!

Persuade him with kindly gifts and gentle words.

—*Homer, 850* B.C.

Persuasion's only shrine is eloquent speech.

—*Aristophanes, 405* B.C.

Part III

ON
PERSEVERANCE
AND
RESOURCEFULNESS

THE · CROW AND THE · PITCHER.

The Crow and the Pitcher

AESOP

A Crow that was extremely thirsty found a pitcher with a little water in it but the water lay so low that he could not come at it. He tried first to break the pitcher, and then to overturn it, but it was both too strong and too heavy for him. He bethought himself however of a device at last that did his business; which was by dropping a great many little pebbles into the water, and raising it that way, till he had it within reach.

Perseverance is more efficacious than violence; and many things that cannot be overcome when they stand together yield themselves up when taken little by little.

—*Sertorius, c.* 80 B.C.

Necessity is the mother of invention.

Skill and patience may succeed where force fails.

Robert Bruce, King of Scotland, and the Spider

SIR WALTER SCOTT

The news of the taking of Castle Kildrummie, the captivity of his wife, and the execution of his brother, reached Robert Bruce, King of Scotland, while he was residing in a miserable cabin on the island of Rachrin, and reduced him to the point of despair.

After receiving this unpleasing news from Scotland, Bruce was lying one morning on his wretched bed, and deliberating with himself whether he had not better resign all thoughts of again attempting to make good his right to the Scottish crown, and, dismissing his followers, transport himself and his brothers to the Holy Land, and spend the rest of his life in fighting against the Saracens. By this he thought, perhaps, he might deserve the forgiveness of Heaven for the great sin of stabbing his enemy Comyn in the church at Dumfries.

But then, on the other hand, he thought it would be both criminal and cowardly to give up his attempts to restore freedom to Scotland, while there yet remained the least chance of his being successful in an undertaking, which, rightly considered, was much more his duty than to drive the infidels out of Palestine, though the superstition of his age might think otherwise.

While he was divided between these reflections, and doubtful of what he should do, Bruce was looking upward to the roof of the cabin in which he lay. His eye was attracted by a spider, which, hanging at the end of a long thread of its own spinning, was endeavoring, as is the fashion of that creature, to swing itself from one beam in the roof to another, for the purpose of fixing the line on which it meant to stretch its web. The insect made the attempt again and again without success; and at length Bruce counted that it had tried to fasten its line six times, and been as often unable to do so.

It came into his head that he had himself fought just six battles against the English and their allies, and that the poor persevering spider was in exactly the same situation with himself, having made as many trials, and been as often disappointed in what it aimed at.

"Now," thought Bruce, "as I have no means of knowing what is best to be done, I will be guided by the luck which shall attend this spider. If the insect shall make another effort to fix its thread, and shall be successful, I will venture a seventh time to try my fortune in Scotland; but if the spider shall fail, I will go to the wars in Palestine, and never return to my native country more."

While Bruce was forming this resolution, the spider made another exertion with all the force it could muster, and succeeded at last in fastening its thread to the beam which it had so often in vain attempted to reach.

Bruce, seeing the success of the spider, resolved to try his own fortune; although he had never before gained a victory, yet he never afterwards sustained any considerable or decisive defeat.

Having determined to renew his efforts to obtain possession of Scotland, notwithstanding the smallness of the means which he had for accomplishing so great a purpose, Bruce removed himself and his followers from Rachrin to the Island of Arran, which lies in the mouth of the Clyde. The King landed, and inquired of the first woman he met, what armed men were in the island. She replied that there had arrived there very lately a body of armed strangers, who had defeated an English officer, the governor of the Castle of Brathwick, had killed him and most of his men, and were now amusing themselves with hunting about the island. The King, having caused himself to be guided to the woods which these strangers most frequented, there blew his horn repeatedly.

Now, the chief of the strangers who had taken the castle, was James Douglas, whom we have already mentioned as one of the best of Bruce's friends, and he was accompanied by some of the bravest of that patriotic band. When he heard Robert Bruce's horn, he knew the sound well, and cried out that yonder was the King, he knew it by his manner of blowing.

So he and his companions hastened to meet King Robert, and there was great joy on both sides; whilst at the same time they could not help weeping when they considered their own forlorn condition, and the great loss that had taken place among their friends since they had last parted. But they were stout-hearted men, and looked forward to freeing their country, in spite of all that had so far happened.

He thought it would be both criminal and cowardly to give up his
    attempts while there yet remained the least chance of being
    successful.

Although he had never before gained a victory, yet he never after-
    wards sustained any considerable or decisive defeat.

They were stout-hearted men, and looked forward to freeing their
    country, in spite of all that had so far happened.

A just man falleth seven times, and riseth up again.
                                        —*Proverbs* 24:16
If at first you don't succeed, try and try again.

Hannibal Mouse and the Other End of the World

EDMUND C. BERKELEY

Once upon a time there was a mouse, and his name was Hannibal Mouse and he lived in Mousetown. He was big and strong, almost grown up, and full of energy, even if he did not do very well in school, and had not learned nearly as much as he should have. He lived with his mother and father, who loved him very much and thought very highly of him—though they realized he had not yet learned, either in or out of school, much that he should have learned by this time.

For several years Hannibal Mouse had been hearing more and more about the big wide world outside of Mousetown. He was tired of Mousetown; he wanted to go away into the big wide world and see what it was like. Also, every now and then, he would hear one mouse say to another, "Right now I would go to the other end of the world for some cheese." Or he would hear a mouse say, "I would go to the other end of the world if you were there."

Hannibal Mouse decided that he wanted to go to the other end of the world more than he wanted to do anything else. The other end of the world sounded very exciting; it seemed to him as if everything he wanted would be there; and he made up his mind "BY MOSH" he would go.

So he talked with his mother and father about going there. They said the other end of the world was rather a long distance away, but they thought it might do him good to see if he could get there. They said to him, "After all, you are a big strong mouse now, even if you aren't yet quite grown-up."

So they gave him a big red bandanna handkerchief for carrying what he needed, and a short stick to go over his shoulder to tie the handkerchief to. Hannibal packed the bandanna handkerchief with a change of shoes and socks to avoid blisters, and a big piece of cheese wrapped in a husk of corn, and a big sunflower leaf to use as an umbrella if it should rain. Then he decided that was plenty to carry. Early the next morning, with the sun shining brightly, he said goodbye to his mother and father; and off he went full of happiness and excitement—he was on his way to the Other End of the World!

He walked to the great road that ran east and west by Mouse-town, and there stopped for a moment, wondering which direction to take. He was sorry he had not thought of obtaining directions, but he had been so sure the first thing he would see would be a sign saying, "To the Other End of the World." He did see a sign, in two parts. One part pointed west and said "To North Goose-port." The other part pointed east and said "To South Catville—Danger." Hannibal reflected. He did not want to have anything to do with danger, and the name "South Catville" suggested cats. They were even more unpleasant than danger. So he chose west.

Having chosen, he promptly convinced himself that his choice was correct, and he set off walking with long strides, with the sun shining warm on his back, and showing all the lovely landscape in front of him, and he did not have a care in the world. He was confident he would soon see another sign that would say, "To the Other End of the World: Best Route."

He walked and walked and walked. The sun rose in the bright blue sky, little white clouds blew above him, and all around him were trees covered with green leaves, and here and there little birds singing in them. The road went on and on, through fields, and woods, and forest, and began climbing through hills. Hannibal felt very happy. At last he was on his way to the Other End of the World!

By and by he met a rabbit, and spoke to him politely and said, "Hi, Mr. Rabbit, this is the way to the Other End of the World,

isn't it?" The Rabbit stopped and looked at Hannibal; then the
Rabbit laughed saying, "What a funny question!" and ran off.
This puzzled Hannibal, but he said to himself, "What an im-
polite rabbit!" and on he went.

Some time in the afternoon he met a dog, and spoke to him
politely, and said, "Hi, Mr. Dog, this is the way to the Other End
of the World, isn't it?" The dog stopped and looked at Hannibal,
and then coughed and yawned, and started to go away; and then
the dog turned his head and said over his shoulder, "Any way is as
good as any other way," and off he went.

This mystified Hannibal Mouse even more, but he kept on walking west with great determination, in spite of a small worry that
had begun nibbling inside of him. What if this road were not the
way to the Other End of the World?

But anyway he was going farther and farther away from Mousetown, which was a great advantage; and certainly he must be coming nearer and nearer to North Gooseport, whatever place that
was, for the sign had said so; and North Gooseport ought to be
closer to the Other End of the World than Mousetown.

The sun set, the sky began to grow dark, Hannibal stopped, ate
some of his cheese, crawled under a bush, lay down, pulled some
of last year's dead leaves over his weary body, said to himself,
"How exciting this is," shut his eyes, and in a little while was fast
asleep.

When morning came, the day was cloudy. The sun shone once
in a while through the clouds. Hannibal got up, stretched, ate a
little more of his cheese, and set off again along the same road.
The road began to wind more and go up over higher hills, and
finally about midafternoon, the road came down again from the
hills into a broad and level stretch of country. There ahead of him
in the distance, he saw something he had never seen before,
though he had read about it, a large city. That must be North
Gooseport, he said to himself.

In the late afternoon he met a rooster. The rooster was sitting
on a fence crowing. He said to the rooster politely, "Hi, Mr.
Rooster, this is the way to the Other End of the World, isn't it?"
The rooster replied crowing "Ur, ur-ur, urrr—All I am interested
in is this end of the world—ur, ur-ur, urr."

Hannibal began to be altogether bothered about the lack of
answers to his main question, but he kept on walking.

By now, Hannibal was tired and no longer happy. The daylight was fading; he had blisters on his feet in spite of changing to the other shoes and socks; and he was hungry—hungry for something better than just cheese. But all he had was cheese and no longer very much of that.

Finally, after eating, he found another bush, and went to sleep under it. But soon after dark, roaring sounds wakened him and the ground trembled. Although he had never seen trains previously, he realized that he must be quite near a railroad; he was frightened. In fact several big trains went by during the night, and Hannibal lost much sleep.

At last morning came, but not before he had heard, several times during the night, the "Whoo! Whoo! Whoo!" of an owl somewhere nearby. When he opened his eyes and looked out from under the bush, he saw that the sky was completely clouded over. He couldn't see the sun anywhere; he could no longer tell which direction to proceed in. Now and then rain came down. The sunflower leaf proved to be no good as an umbrella. When he held it over his head some of the rain came through holes in the leaf, and some more rain ran down into his sleeve. It was a plain nuisance; so he just threw it away.

Hannibal realized as he looked at the fields and back roads around him that he no longer had any idea which direction to take. He was lost. He was wet. He was discouraged. He was weary. He was altogether miserable.

But he saw in the distance, in the opposite direction from the railroad, some tall oak trees. He said to himself, "Perhaps that owl that I heard in the night might be over there, and he might be a wise owl, and maybe he would help me."

So he walked through several fields over to the oak trees. Searching among the trees, he finally found a very tall tree with a hole in it; and there in the hole, sure enough, was an owl sitting with his eyes closed. By now it was drizzling steadily.

Hannibal called up to the owl. He said, "Please, Mr. Owl, will you help me? I want to go to the Other End of the World? Could you please tell me the right direction?"

The owl opened one eye and said, "Whoo-whoo-whoo-are you?"

The mouse said, "I am Hannibal Mouse from Mousetown."

"Oh," said the owl. "And what are you doing here, 20 miles away from Mousetown?"

Hannibal said, "I am on my way to the Other End of the World. I have been traveling steadily for two days and living on cheese, which is almost gone, and I ought to be quite near to the Other End of the World by now."

The owl smiled and said, "Young mouse, do you know how big the world is?"

"Well," said Hannibal Mouse, "I know it is rather big, but after all I have been traveling steadily for two days. I ought to have gone a good part of the way."

The owl said, "Young mouse, do you know how long it would take you to travel to the other end of the world and back again at 10 miles a day?"

"No," said Hannibal Mouse, "I didn't find that out from anybody."

"Well," said the owl, "it is time you did, young mouse. To go to the other end of the world at that rate would take you three years —three years to walk all the way around the world to the other end of the world—and then it would take you three years to walk back."

The owl paused, and added, "Even if there was a road, and there isn't." The owl paused again and added, "Even if the other end of the world were one and the same place."

"Oh!" said Hannibal Mouse, "why didn't anybody tell me it would take three years?"

The owl said, "Did you ask anybody how far it was?"

"Yes," said Hannibal Mouse, "I talked to my mother and father about the Other End of the World. They said it was a long way but they thought it would do me good to try and get there. That is just what they said."

"A long way!" said the owl with scorn in his voice. "How long is 'a long way'? You did not find out how far it was. You did not ask enough questions, young mouse."

"Oh!" said Hannibal, who was still appalled at the "three years."

He sat down on the ground at the foot of the owl's tree, and started thinking about what he might do. This was a great effort for Hannibal, who was not accustomed to thinking.

His first impulse was to turn around and start home. But that would mean giving up. Most certainly he did not want to go home

—and be laughed at, not by his mother and father, who were kind, but by all the other mice in Mousetown. And he did not want to give up. The Other End of the World was important to him; he really wanted to get there. "BY MOSH" he would not give up!

Yet walking for three years to get to the Other End of the World, and then back again for three more years, was impossible. Furthermore, the owl had said he could not get there by walking. Perhaps that meant he might be able to get there some other way, not by walking. Maybe there was a way to go to the Other End of the World much faster than walking.

If he could only find out some more information—if he could only find out a better way to go to the Other End of the World— if he could only discover why his questions were answered by all the animals with conundrums: "What a funny question!" "Any way is as good as any other way." "Who cares about the other end of the world!" "Even if the other end of the world were one and the same place."

Finally, he spoke up again, "Mr. Owl, is there any place nearby where I can find out a lot of information quickly—a library, a school, or something?"

The owl opened one eye, looked down once more, and said, "Young mouse, daytime is sleeptime for me. Go to the edge of the field over there and look for Mrs. Hedgehog, and see if she can help you."

So Hannibal went in the direction the owl had pointed out. He came to the edge of the field, where there was a kind of hedge made of rocks, bushes, and small trees in a line between that field and the next field. He found a path leading into the hedge, and soon he came to a door, and on the door was a sign, "Mrs. Hilda Hedgehog—Library, School." He knocked on the door.

In a moment it opened and there in front of him was a nice-looking lady hedgehog with a fresh gray apron.

"Please, Mrs. Hedgehog," said Hannibal, "I need some information. I am trying to go to the Other End of the World. I have found out I do not know enough to get there. I need lots of information quickly. I need to read in your library—perhaps I need to go to your school to learn more."

Mrs. Hedgehog smiled at the frankness with which Hannibal spoke. She saw he looked tired and wet and hungry. So she said to him, "Young mouse, come in and let me give you something to eat, and tell me just what you are trying to do."

So Hannibal entered and told her his whole story, while she listened; and she fed him cheese, and freshly baked bread, and some celery and for dessert some very delicious acorns. Hannibal began to feel as if the big wide world outside of Mousetown was a nice place after all. When Hannibal finished, Mrs. Hedgehog said, "I suggest that you come to my school for a couple of weeks, and let me teach you the information you need. But you will have to work to earn your keep, and the cost of the teaching."

Hannibal said, "All right, I will."

After a good night's sleep in one of Mrs. Hedgehog's rooms, while the rain came down outside, he got up early and spent three hours working for Mrs. Hedgehog: cleaning, cutting wood, stacking it in the shed, and after the rain stopped, searching for acorns and other nuts to replenish the supplies of the school.

In the afternoon he attended school run by Mrs. Hedgehog. At school there were several squirrels, chipmunks, hedgehogs, field mice, and a guinea pig learning the ins and outs of hedgerows. They were learning how to scamper, how to observe, how to think logically, and how to be completely still, become almost invisible, and blend with their surroundings. There was a special course for Hannibal in geography and transportation. Hannibal received a globe, many maps, timetables, and travel folders, to be studied.

School continued for a couple of weeks. By the end of that time Hannibal had found out and decided just what he wanted to do; he wanted to go to Southralia, which was actually at the opposite end of the globe from Mousetown; and there he wanted to ride with the Jumping Kangaroos. He had found out there were regular trips to Southralia by Flying Gooseways. They could easily transport a mouse and his red bandanna baggage.

In those two weeks Hannibal earned his roundtrip fare, which was not great for a mouse's weight, by hunting for nuts and selling them to the squirrels who lived here and there in the hedge and nearby woods. They really wanted the nuts and would pay a good price for them, and Hannibal had sharp eyes.

He made arrangements to fly to Southralia on the next trip of Flying Gooseways.

The day for departure came. He said a fond goodbye to Mrs. Hedgehog, thanked her for all the help she had been to him, paid all that he owed, and gave her an unexpectedly large supply of acorns for her school stores. She was most pleased.

He went down to the North Gooseport station, and climbed onto the back of Number Three Goose, where he stowed himself deep in the feathers in the middle of the back, with just his head out. The goose convoy took off soon afterwards, and Hannibal quickly found himself half a mile high in the sky, flying at several hundred miles an hour, in vee formation. It was very exciting. The sun set and at dark he fell asleep. But the big goose convoy kept on flying all through the night. The next morning his goose told him they were very near Southralia, and soon would be landing.

Shortly afterwards, in bright sunlight, the convoy came down at South Gooseport in Southralia. Hannibal Mouse climbed off Number Three Goose, collected his red bandanna baggage, and set off in search of the Great Herd of Kangaroos.

After several small adventures, he found the Great Herd of Kangaroos some miles away. He stood patiently at the edge of the Kangaroo Meadow, waiting. Finally, one of the lady kangaroos with a little one in her pouch noticed the red bandanna and came over to see who was there. Hannibal Mouse spoke up, introduced himself and said, "Mrs. Kangaroo, I have come from the other end of the world, Mousetown near North Gooseport in Northeria. My main purpose in coming to Southralia is to ride, if I may, in the pouch of a kangaroo. I think this would be a fantastic experience."

"Well," said Mrs. Kangaroo, "you flatter me, young mouse— Hannibal—it is nothing to get excited about really. I'll ask this youngster Roo to move over a bit and you can climb in my pouch. I'll be delighted."

Hannibal Mouse was overjoyed. He climbed in next to little Roo. For many hours on that day and the next day he rode hither and thither with Mrs. Kangaroo on her great jumps.

This was far more exciting to Hannibal even than the trip over the ocean, on the back of Number Three Goose. He was close to the ground during the jumps, so close that it was almost frightening.

It was an activity much more full of sensation than the almost still experience of flying half a mile high in the air on the back of a goose.

Finally, he said goodbye to his Kangaroo friends, and returned on the Flying Gooseways to North Gooseport in Northeria. He took with him many memories, his baggage in the red bandanna, and picture postcards of the wonderful sights in Southralia.

After landing in North Gooseport, he set out walking to Mousetown. At the end of two days—twice as long as it had taken Flying Gooseways to fly him from Southralia to North Gooseport—he arrived back at Mousetown.

His mother and father welcomed him, and said, "My heavens, you have been gone four weeks. You're still alive! How wonderful! We were so afraid a cat had caught you. Tell us your adventures." So he told them all that had happened. They hardly knew whether to believe him or not. But he brought out his postcards, and showed them, and they believed him. And from that day to this, when someone in Mousetown says, "I'll go to the other end of the world," the answer is "Like Hannibal Mouse!"

He was sorry he had not thought of obtaining directions.

Having chosen, he promptly convinced himself his choice was correct.

Cats were even more unpleasant than danger.

"Any way is as good as any other way."

But anyhow he was going farther and farther away from home, and that was a great advantage.

"I have been traveling steadily for two days, and I ought to be quite near to the Other End of the World by now."

"They said it was a long way but they thought it would do me good to try to get there."

"A long way! How long is 'a long way'? You did not ask enough questions, young mouse."

He began to feel that the big wide world outside of his home town was a nice place after all.

It was an activity more full of sensation and excitement than anything he had ever before experienced.

When Hannibal Mouse started on his journey, he lacked a good deal of common sense. Especially, he lacked the minimum amount of knowledge he should have acquired in school. But he compensated for his deficiencies by learning more information when he needed to; by making definite his vague objective; and by earning the resources needed to carry out his journey. Basically, he succeeded because he persevered, found out what he needed to know, and overcame the real obstacles he encountered. This is rather a good recipe for success.

The Fly, the Spider, and the Hornet

EDMUND C. BERKELEY

Once a Fly, a Spider, and a Hornet were trapped inside a window screen in an attic. For several hours they walked up and down, left and right, here and there, all over the screen. They could look through the screen at the summer woods, feel the summer breezes, and smell the summer smells; but they could not find any hole to pass through the screen to the woods and fields, so tantalizingly close, yet so far away.

Finally, they decided to hold a conference on the problem of getting through the screen.

The Fly spoke first and said, "My Colleagues, I have surveyed this screen for many hours without finding any hole. But I cannot believe that there is no hole in this screen. All my experience of the world up to the present time has shown me that there are holes in thickets of twigs, holes in screens of leaves, holes in tangles of grass, holes everywhere. In fact, I have been able to fly over, under, or around every barrier I have ever encountered. Nature does not make thickets, screens, and tangles without holes.

"Therefore, the principle to be used is perseverance in spite of obstacles. I will fly again and again and again at the screen in hopes of getting through. As the old saying goes, 'If at first you don't succeed, try and try again.' I'll never give up; my honor as a Fly is at stake."

The Spider spoke second and said: "My Colleagues, I too have surveyed this screen for many hours without finding any hole. I am sorry I have to contradict my honorable Colleague the Fly, but I have come to the conclusion that this screen has no hole.

"Therefore, the principle to be used is adjustment to changed conditions. So I will plan to spend the rest of my life inside this screen. I shall build my web inside the screen, catch my food, and live out my life in this new way."

The Hornet spoke third, and said, "My Colleagues, I too have persistently surveyed this screen for many hours without finding any hole. But I remember that I flew into this general region without going through that screen. Accordingly, there must be some other way of returning to the woods and the fields.

"Therefore, the principle to be used is exploration of other alternatives. I shall stop my fruitless search for a hole in this screen, and instead search in other directions and avenues to find other means of escape."

The Fly and the Spider said at once, "Honorable Colleague, please pardon us for saying so, but that is plain silly. Just think how close you are to escaping through the screen—only a few little thin wires between you and freedom."

The Hornet replied, "My friends, those wires may be few, and little, and thin, but nevertheless they are too substantial for me to pass through."

The Fly then said, "Besides, honorable Colleague, this conference of ours was called on the subject of getting through the screen—and, honorable Colleague, you are off the subject and out of order." The Spider said, "I must agree with the Fly."

Thereupon, the Hornet made a motion that the subject of the conference be amended from getting through the screen to escaping to the woods and fields. But he was outvoted 2 to 1.

None of the three would change his views, and the conference soon adjourned.

A day later, the Fly died of exhaustion.

A week later, the Spider, having caught only one moth in his web, died of starvation.

But an hour later, the Hornet exploring under the eaves of the roof between the inclined beams of the attic, found an opening to the outdoors, and flew out, returning to a long life in the woods and fields.

Nature does not make thickets, screens, and tangles without holes.
The principle to be used is perseverance in spite of obstacles.
This screen has no hole.
The principle to be used is adjustment to changed conditions.
There must be some other way than through this screen.
The principle to be used is exploration of other alternatives.

The good huntsman must follow the hounds, and not give up the
    chase.
                            —*Plato*, c. 375 B.C.
If it be the right way, advance; if it be the wrong way, retire.
                            —*Lao-tsze*, c. 550 B.C.
There are more ways than one of cooking a goose.
                            —*Ione Shriber*, 1941
To overcome an obstacle, it is often necessary to understand it.
When a method for overcoming an obstacle fails again and again,
    the method should no longer be assumed correct.

Part IV

BEHAVIOR–
MORAL
AND
OTHERWISE

A Small Wharf of Stones

BENJAMIN FRANKLIN

I had a strong inclination for the sea, but my father declared against it; however, living near the water, I was much in and about it, learnt early to swim well, and to manage boats; and when in a boat or canoe with other boys, I was commonly allowed to govern, especially in any case of difficulty; and upon other occasions I was generally a leader among the boys, and sometimes led them into scrapes, of which I will mention one instance, as it shows an early projecting public spirit, tho' not then justly conducted.

There was a salt-marsh that bounded part of the mill-pond, on the edge of which, at high water, we used to stand to fish for minnows. By much trampling, we had made it a mere quagmire. My proposal was to build a wharf there fit for us to stand upon, and I showed my comrades a large heap of stones, which were intended for a new house near the marsh, and which would very well suit our purpose. Accordingly, in the evening, when the workmen were gone, I assembled a number of my play-fellows, and working with them diligently like so many emmets, sometimes two or three to a stone, we brought them all away and built our little wharf.

The next morning the workmen were surprised at missing the stones, which were found in our wharf.

Inquiry was made after the removers; we were discovered and complained of; several of us were corrected by our fathers; and, though I pleaded the usefulness of the work, mine convinced me that nothing was useful which was not honest.

One may go wrong in many different ways, but right only in one.
—*Aristotle, c.* 335 B.C.

A hundred steps in the right direction will not atone for one step
    in the wrong direction.
                                                —*Chinese proverb*
How you get it, that is the question, by right or wrong.
                                                —*Plautus, c. 200* B.C.
Though I pleaded the usefulness of my work, my father convinced
    me that nothing was useful which was not honest.
                                                —*Benjamin Franklin, 1737*
To be ready and willing to change one's mind upon obtaining
    good evidence for doing so, is the pathway to achievement.

The Three Bricklayers

E. C. B.

Once I saw three men laying bricks.
I asked the first one, "What are you doing?"
He said, "Can't you see? I am laying bricks."
I asked the second one, "What are you doing?"
He said, "I am making a good straight wall—see?"
I asked the third one, "What are you doing?"
He said, "I am building a cathedral."

The sight of a man hath the force of a lion.
                                                —*George Herbert, 1640*
The greatest thing a human soul ever does in this world is to see
    something.
                                                —*John Ruskin, 1850*
Where there is no vision, the people perish.
                                                —*Proverbs 29:18*

The Good Samaritan

ST. LUKE, 10:25–37

And behold, a certain lawyer stood up and tempted him, saying, Master, what shall I do to inherit eternal life?

And he said unto him, What is written in the law? how readest thou?

And he answering said, Thou shalt love the Lord thy God with all thy heart, and with all thy soul, and with all thy strength, and with all thy mind; and thy neighbor as thyself.

And he said unto him, Thou hast answered right: this do, and thou shalt live.

But he, desiring to justify himself, said unto Jesus, And who is my neighbor?

Jesus made answer and said, A certain man was going down from Jerusalem to Jericho; and he fell among robbers, which both stripped him and beat him, and departed, leaving him half dead.

And by chance a certain priest was going down that way: and when he saw him, he passed by on the other side.

And in like manner a Levite also, when he came to the place, and saw him, passed by on the other side.

But a certain Samaritan, as he journeyed, came where he was: and when he saw him, he was moved with compassion,

And came to him, and bound up his wounds, pouring on them oil and wine; and he set him on his own beast, and brought him to an inn, and took care of him.

And on the morrow he took out two pence, and gave them to the host, and said, Take care of him; and whatsoever thou spendest more, I, when I come back again, will repay thee.

Which of these three, thinkest thou, proved neighbor unto him that fell among the robbers?

And he said, He that shewed mercy on him. And Jesus said unto him, Go, and do thou likewise.

Wide and sweet and glorious is compassion.

—*A. C. Swinburne, 1878*

The quality of mercy is not strain'd;
It droppeth as the gentle rain from heaven
Upon the place beneath; it is twice blest;
It blesseth him that gives, and him that takes.

—*Shakespeare, 1597*

Much Obliged, Dear Lord

FULTON OURSLER

Her name was Anna Maria Cecily Sophia Virginia Avalon Thessalonians.

She was born into slavery on the Eastern Shore of Maryland, and her earthly master had thought it a great joke to saddle the little brown baby with that ungainly christening.

As a young girl, in the first year of her freedom, Ann helped the doctor the day my mother was born. That was in 1866. Twenty-seven years later she was in the bedroom when I was born. She gave me my first bath, but that was not all she gave me.

I remember her as she sat at the kitchen table in our house, the hard old brown hands folded across her starched wrapper, the glistening black eyes lifted to the whitewashed ceiling, and the husky old whispering voice saying:

"Much obliged, dear Lord, for my vittles."

"Ann," I asked, "what is a vittle?"

"It's what I've got to eat and drink—that's vittles."

"But you'd get your vittles whether you thanked the Lord or not."

"Sure. But it makes everything taste better to be thankful. In some people's religion the whole family does it every meal, but not my church. So I do it just for myself."

After the meal was over she thanked the Lord again and then lit her clay pipe with reedy stem; to this day, every smoking pipe I smell makes me think of my old nurse.

"You know," she said, blowing expert rings in the direction of the kitchen range, "it's a funny thing about being thankful—it's a game an old colored preacher taught me to play. It's looking for things to be thankful for. You don't know how many of them you pass right by, unless you go looking for them.

"Take this morning, for instance. I wake up and I lay there, lazy-like, wondering what I got to be thankful for now. And you know what? I can't think of anything. Tee-hee! What must the good God think of me, His child? But it's the honest truth—I just can't think of a thing to thank Him for.

"And then, what you think? My daughter, Josie, comes opening the bedroom door, and right straight from the kitchen comes the most delicious morning smell that ever tickled my old nose. Coffee! Much obliged, dear Lord, for the coffee and the daughter to have it ready for an old woman when she wakes up. Much obliged, dear Lord, for the smell of it—and for the way it puts ambition even into me. Some people try to tell me coffee is bad, but I've been drinking it for fifty years now and I'm obliged to the dear Lord for every cup I get.

"Now for a while I've got to help Josie with the housework. It's a little hard to find anything to thank God for in housework; your ma will tell you the same thing, and so will any other woman. But when I come to the mantelpiece to dust the ornaments, there's the Little Boy Blue. How long you think I've had that little china boy? Since before your mother was born. I was a slave when I got it for Christmas. But I never broke it—never even got it chipped. There he sits, all shiny blue, on the mantel, with his golden horn to his mouth. I love that little boy; he's been with me all the time; he's my little mantelpiece brother. Much obliged, dear Lord, for Little Boy Blue.

"And almost everything I touch with the dustrag reminds me of something I love to remember. Even the pictures that hang on the walls. It's like a visit with my folks, here and yonder. Funny, when you get to my age you've got as many of your folks up there as down here. The pictures look at me and I look at them and I remember so much that's good. I get through my housework before I know what I'm doing, I've been so busy remembering.

"You go downtown and look in the windows. So many pretty things . . ."

"But, Ann," I broke in. "You can't buy them. You haven't got enough money."

"I've always had enough money for what I want. I don't want those pretty things. What I want a long velvet gown for, trailing halfway behind? But I think it's pretty, and I love to stand there and play dolls. Yes, I do. I play dolls in my mind, and I think of your ma, and your aunt Dot, and your cousin Leona—how each of them would look in that dress—and I have a lot of fun at that window. I'm much obliged to the dear Lord for playing in my mind, old as I am; it's a kind of happiness.

"Once I got caught in the rain. My daughter Josie thought I would catch my death. Tee-hee! It was fun for me. I always heard about fancy people's shower baths. Now I had me one and it was wonderful. That cool water dropping on my cheeks was just exactly like a baby's fingers—and I always loved them.

"You know, God just is giving heaven away to people all day long. I've been to Druid Hill Park and seen the gardens. But you know what? I likes the old bush in your back yard a sight better. One rose will fill your nose with all the sweetness you can stand. . . ."

Now Ann must have told me these things at different times, but they have ranged themselves in my memory as one long, husky whispered monologue. For many a year I forgot she had ever said them.

It was not until trouble had clamped down on me with a throttle hold and my old ego had been battered. An hour came when I recognized danger in my own sense of despair. I searched my memory as a bankrupt frantically pokes through safe-deposit boxes, looking for a morsel of counsel. Ann had been a long time moldering in her grave, but her rumbling half-whispered tones came back to me, with the game she taught me at the kitchen table of searching out every cause for thankfulness.

I urged myself to play that game. . . . I was in the subway at the time, vile-smelling and over-crowded, and it happened there was a burst of laughter that, probably because I was seeking it, reminded me that sorrow passes. . . . And I looked about me and marked a young girl's eyes shining with hope for the evening; and again, pride in reading of a batsman's home run bringing a glow to the face of a tired old clerk. . . . And when I went up on the street, clean snow was falling; a church was lighted and its open doorway called to me. I went in. And I knelt. And my heart filled with warmth when I began to count over my many gifts, my many blessings. How much—how overpoweringly much—I had to be grateful for.

For work to be done—good work that I could put my heart into —for that I'm much obliged, dear Lord. For the ability to take care of those who look to me. For my loved ones, who love me more than I deserve. For friends—so many who had reached out or spoken, or who had mercifully kept silent in my troubles. And for utter strangers, whom I knew now God had sent to me in my trial, miraculously on hand to help. . . . I found the words of thanks tumbling from my lips and heard myself thanking God for difficulties, because they renewed my faith. . . .

There's magic in thanksgiving. You may begin with a cup of coffee, but once you start, the gratefulness swells and the causes multiply. Finally, it seems the more you thank the more you have, and the more you get to be thankful for—and, of course, that's the whole spiritual keystone.

The soul of long-dead Ann was a big soul—big enough to see God everywhere. I shall never be as big a soul as she was, but she taught me. The word came from the dingy street where she lived in East Baltimore with Josie, her daughter, that Ann was dying. I remember Mother drove me there in a cab. I stood by Ann's bedside; she was in deep pain, and the hard old hands were knotted together in a desperate clutch. Poor old woman—what had she to be thankful for now?

She opened her eyes and looked at us; her eyes lingered with mine.

"Much obliged, dear Lord," she said, "for such fine friends."

She never spoke again—except in my heart. But there she speaks every day. I'm much obliged to God for that.

It makes everything taste better to be thankful.

So I do it just for myself.

It's a game an old colored preacher taught me to play. It's looking for things to be thankful for. You don't know how many of them pass you by unless you go looking for them.

When you get to my age, you've got as many of your folks up there as down here.

I've always had enough money for what I want.

I'm much obliged to the dear Lord for playing in my mind, old as I am; it's a kind of happiness.

One rose can fill your nose with all the sweetness you can stand.

A burst of laughter reminded me that sorrow passes.

It seems that the more you thank, the more you have, and the more you get to be thankful for—and of course that's the whole spiritual keystone.

"Much obliged, dear Lord, for such fine friends."

The Fisherman, the Farmer, and the Peddler

EDMUND C. BERKELEY

The sun was shining in a blue sky; the leaves on the trees were new and green; and little white clouds blew from the west, on a bright summer morning. Leal Merimedon was walking down the long, white, sandy road, on his usual quest for adventures.

As he walked around a turn in the road, he came to an inlet from the sea. There was a beach, and an old wharf, with a shed by the wharf, and a small house. Tied to the wharf was an old fishing boat with a mast and a sail. The sail was gray; but it had two patches of red cloth in it. White gulls were circling in the air. The tide was out, showing sandy flats. Sitting on the wharf in the sunshine was a fisherman mending a net.

Leal Merimedon came near and smiled.

The fisherman looked up and smiled at him, and said, "Hi, stranger, I've some nice fish, caught yesterday. Buy some?"

Leal sat down on the wharf edge and said, "Yes, I'd like some of your fish. Show them to me."

The fisherman walked into the shed and brought back a pail holding a silvery mackerel. Leal bought the fish, put it in his pack, and then he said:

"How long have you fished here?"

"Oh, from the time I was fifteen until now, that's thirty years," said the fisherman. "I have caught a lot of fish for people, and for those gulls, too," he said, pointing. "They eat all the parts of the fish that people won't—and they keep this little bay clean."

"Will you ever stop fishing?" said Leal.

"No," said the fisherman. "I don't think so."

"Do you ever want to do something else?" said Leal.

"No," said the fisherman. "I've had a good life. I never know what my net will catch, much or little, and I take the good and the bad together."

They talked a little more; then Leal wished him well, and walked on down the road.

Around another curve in the road, Leal Merimedon came to a farm. It had three wide fields, a big red barn, and a small white farmhouse. In the paddock there were a horse and two cows. The top of the barn was filled with hay. On either side of the farmhouse were two great pine trees that towered into the sky, and breezes whispered through their pine needles.

On the porch of the farmhouse, a grizzled farmer was sitting with a churn, making butter out of cream. The farmer looked at Leal and said, "Hi, stranger. I've some good corn. Buy some?"

"Yes," said Leal Merimedon. "I'd like some of your corn." The farmer put down the churn, wiped his hands on his trousers, strode into the barn, and came back with two great ears of fresh yellow corn, and gave them to Leal Merimedon, who paid for them. Then Leal sat on the edge of the porch and said:

"How long have you farmed here?"

"Most of my life, from the time I was fifteen until now, that's forty years," said the farmer, going on with his churning. "I've had good health; I've made many changes on this farm. The fences are mended; the crops are growing; the stock is well fed. Now is lay-by time, and so I can churn today while my wife goes to market."

"Will you ever stop farming?" said Leal.

"No," said the farmer. "I like it here."

"Do you ever want to do something else?" said Leal.

"No," said the farmer. "I have had a good life. I have seen so much grow and bloom and fruit on my farm. When I first came here, many of the fields were in weeds. But I have ploughed, and farmed, and cultivated; and the farm is a much better property now than it was when I was young. I have been happy here; I have built much and planted much, and I have much more still to do."

They talked a little more; then Leal wished him well, and walked off down the road.

Leal walked some distance farther, and then by the side of the road he came upon a great peach tree loaded with big ripe pink and yellow peaches. And under the tree was a large pack and next to it seemingly lying asleep was an old man with a weatherbeaten face and snow-white hair.

Leal came up to the tree, and looked at the peaches; they smelled ripe and delicious. As he stretched out his hand towards the peach tree, the old man opened his eyes and smiled, and sat up.

"Hi, stranger," he said. "Take some of the peaches. They are good, and they don't cost anything."

"Are they your peaches?" said Leal.

"Yes, in a way," said the old man. "I planted this tree years and years ago."

"What do you do?" said Leal.

"I am a peddler, and a poet, and a sower of seeds," said the old man. "All my life I have been wandering here and there, peddling this and that, talking to people, and listening to what they say, and planting peach stones."

"Why do you plant peach stones?" said Leal.

"Well," said the old man, "Once when I was fifteen—that's sixty years ago—I was climbing a hill in the deep woods. I came upon a peach tree covered with ripe peaches. I tasted the peaches. They were the most delicious peaches that I had ever eaten. So then and there I made up my mind that I would go here and there all through the world and plant the seeds of that peach tree."

"And now," said the old man, "wherever I go in my wandering, I find that the peach trees I planted are growing; they bear peaches at many seasons, and all of them bring delight to thousands and thousands of people who eat the peaches."

"Will you ever stop doing this?" said Leal.

"Yes," said the old man, "when I am dead. It won't be too long now. Some days now I just have to sleep most of the day. But I am very happy and very content. The world is a different world and a better world because I have lived. I have made thousands of peach trees grow where there were none before."

"You said you were a poet," said Leal Merimedon.

"Not much of one," said the old man, "but here is one of my poems:

> A dry November day splits wide the milkweed's pod;
> The sleeping silky seeds awake;
>   Each spreads its parachute;
> Away into the frosty air
> They blow on puffs of wind.
> Their former stalk is left behind,
>   Stark and destitute.
>
> Some seeds stall in the dead autumn grass;
> Some catch in the leafless branches nearby;
> Some sail far down the meadow,
>   Out of sight,
> Into a new and fertile land.
> So spread the thoughts of men.

"It's not a very good poem," said the old man. "But milkweed seeds, peach stones, thoughts—they are all rather much the same thing."

Leal smiled. The old man's face was calm and thoughtful; his eyes were looking into the distance; his mind was elsewhere.

Leal Merimedon ate his second peach in silence; then he wished the old man well, and continued down the long, white sandy road.

I never know what my net will catch, much or little, and I take the
    good and the bad together

I have been happy here; I have built much and I have planted
   much, and I have much more still to do.
Wherever I go in my wandering, I find that the peach trees that I
   planted are growing; they bear peaches at many seasons; and
   all of them bring delight to thousands of people who eat the
   peaches.
I am very happy and very content. The world is a different world
   and a better world because I have lived.
I have made thousands of peach trees grow where there were none
   before.

> The sleeping silky seeds awake;
> Each spreads its parachute;
>   Away into the frosty air
> \ They blow on puffs of wind. . . .
> So spread the thoughts of men.

The value of life lies not in the length of days but in the use we
   make of them; a man may live long, yet live very little. Satis-
   faction in life depends not on the number of your years, but
   on your will.
                              —*Montaigne*, 1580
Live all you can; it is a mistake not to.
                              —*Henry James*, 1903
It is not wise, believe me, to say "Tomorrow I shall live"; too late
   is tomorrow's life. Live today.
                              —*Martial*, A.D. 85
To know how to live is my trade and my art.
                              —*Montaigne*, 1580
While your life is still in its flowering spring time, see that you
   use it. Its feet are not slow as it glides away.
                              —*Tibullus, c.* B.C. 17
I warmed both hands before the fire of life;
   It sinks and I am ready to depart.
                              —*Walter Savage Landor, c.* 1850

The measure of life is its excellence not its length.
                                        —*Plutarch*, A.D. 95
Wish not so much to live long as to live well.
                                    —*Benjamin Franklin, 1738*

Part V

THE
PROBLEM
OF
TRUTH

On Being a Reasonable Creature

BENJAMIN FRANKLIN

I believe I have omitted mentioning that, in my first voyage from Boston, being becalm'd off Block Island, our people set about catching cod, and hauled up a great many. Hitherto I had stuck to my resolution of not eating animal food, and on this occasion I consider'd, with my master Tryon, the taking every fish as a kind of unprovoked murder, since none of them had, or ever could do us any injury that might justify the slaughter. All this seemed very reasonable.

But I had formerly been a great lover of fish, and, when this came hot out of the frying-pan, it smelt admirably well. I balanc'd some time between principle and inclination, till I recollected that, when the fish were opened, I saw smaller fish taken out of their stomachs; then thought I, "If you eat one another, I don't see why we mayn't eat you." So I din'd upon cod very heartily, and continued to eat with other people, returning only now and then occasionally to a vegetable diet.

So convenient a thing is it to be a *reasonable creature*, since it enables one to find or make a reason for every thing one has a mind to do.

Men freely believe what they wish to believe.
                    —*Julius Caesar, c.* 52 B.C.
With how much ease believe we what we wish.
                    —*John Dryden,* 1677
What ardently we wish, we soon believe.
                    —*Edward Young,* 1744
Truth is rarely pure and never simple.
                    —*Oscar Wilde* (1854–1900)
So convenient a thing it is to be a reasonable creature, since it

enables one to find or make a reason for everything one has a mind to do.

—*Benjamin Franklin, c. 1750*

The Monkey and the Spectacles

IVAN A. KRYLOFF

Once a Monkey in his old age became far-sighted. He had heard men say that this misfortune was not important, if one used spectacles.

So he obtained half a dozen pairs of spectacles and tried them. He turned them this way and that way, put them on the top of his head, fastened them to his tail, smelled them, licked them. Still the spectacles produced no improvement in his sight.

Finally, he cried, "What fools they are who listen to the nonsense that men utter! I have been told nothing but lies about spectacles." Then he threw them hard upon a stone, so that they were shattered.

Moral: We speak ill of things we do not understand.

A fool who thinks himself wise is a fool indeed.

—*Dhammapala, c. 425* B.C.

Fools cannot understand clever men.

—*Vauvenargues, 1746*

The world is as full of fools as a tree is full of leaves.

—*G. B. Shaw, 1904*

Don't play the lute before a donkey.

—*Justus Doolittle, 1872*

The finest paintings are useless to a man who cannot see.

The Golden Trumpets
of Yap Yap

MIKE QUIN

The famous explorer, Dr. Emery Hornsnagle, in his recent book, *Strange Customs of the People of Yap Yap*, makes some interesting observations on the practice of free speech among the inhabitants of that little-known island.

While being entertained in the palace of Iggy Bumbum (High Chief), the Slobob of Yap Yap, Dr. Hornsnagle asked the ruler whether free expression of public sentiment was allowed by the law.

"Yes, indeed," replied the Slobob. "The people of our island have absolute freedom of speech, and the government is conducted in exact conformity to public opinion."

"Just how does that work?" asked Dr. Hornsnagle. "By what method are you able to tell what public opinion thinks about the various matters that come up ?"

"That is very simple," explained the Slobob. "Whenever any policy has to be decided, we assemble the entire population in the large courtyard of the palace. The High Priest then reads from a scroll to inform them of the business at hand. When that is finished, I determine the will of my people by listening to the Golden Trumpets."

"And what are the Golden Trumpets?" asked Hornsnagle.

"Golden Trumpets," said the Slobob, "are the only means by which public opinion may be expressed. I raise my right hand above my head and call out: 'All those in favor blow.' Instantly, all those in favor of the proposed action blow upon Golden Trumpets. Then I raise my left hand and call out: 'All those opposed, blow.' This time the opposition blows Golden Trumpets. The side making the loudest noise is naturally the majority and the issue is decided in their favor."

"That," said Dr. Hornsnagle, "is to my mind the most complete democracy I have ever heard of. I would like very much to witness one of these expressions of public opinion and take some photographs."

On the next afternoon, Dr. Hornsnagle had the opportunity he desired. The people of the whole island were assembled in the palace courtyard to decide an important issue. They numbered about three thousand and were all quite naked except for loin cloths. However, just before the ceremony was about to begin, four richly clothed gentlemen were carried in on bejeweled litters. Glittering with priceless gems and reeking with perfume, they were deposited at the very front of the crowd, where they squatted on silken pillows and were fanned with peacock feathers by attendants.

"Who are they?" asked Hornsnagle.

"They," replied the Slobob, "are the richest men on the island."

Immediately after the arrival of the wealthy class, the High Priest read off his scroll. Then the Slobob stepped forward and raised his right hand.

"All those in favor, blow," he shouted.

The four wealthy citizens all lifted Golden Trumpets and blew lustily.

The Slobob now lifted his left hand. "All those opposed, blow," he shouted. Not a sound came from the giant assemblage. "It is so decided," announced the Slobob, and the affair was over.

Later on, Dr. Hornsnagle asked the Slobob why the four wealthy citizens were the only ones who blew trumpets.

"They are the only ones who can afford to own Golden Trumpets," explained the Slobob. "The rest are only poor working people."

"That doesn't seem very much like free speech to me," remarked Hornsnagle. "All it amounts to is a group of rich men blowing their own horns. In America we have real public expression."

"Is that so?" exclaimed the Slobob. "And how do you do it in America?"

"In America," said Hornsnagle, "instead of having Golden Trumpets, we have newspapers, magazines and radio broadcasting stations."

"That is very interesting," said the Slobob. "But who owns these newspapers, magazines, and broadcasting stations?"

"The rich men," replied Hornsnagle.

"Then it is the same as Yap Yap," said the Slobob. "It is the rich men blowing their own horns that make all the noise."

What I tell you three times is true.
> —*Lewis Carroll* (1832–1898)

Is not the truth the truth?
> —*Shakespeare,* 1598

The truth is bitter and disagreeable to fools; but falsehood is sweet and acceptable.
> —*St. Chrysostom, c.* A.D. 400

A well-intentioned lie is better than a mischief-making truth.
> —*Sadi, c.* 1258

A little truth helps the lie go down.
> —*Italian proverb*

Everything is true in part and false in part.
> —*Pascal,* 1660

Any fool can tell the truth, but it takes a man of some sense to know how to lie well.
> —*Samuel Butler, c.* 1890

It is the rich men blowing their own horns that make all the noise.
> —*Mike Quin,* 1940

The Barrels and the Pittsburgh Manufacturer

EDMUND C. BERKELEY

Once there was a manufacturer in Pittsburgh, whose factory made good strong steel barrels; and he wanted to increase his sales.

So he consulted his advertising agent, and together they worked out and published in the newspaper a dramatic advertisement showing how strong the barrels were, using a photograph of an elephant standing on one of the barrels and the slogan "Barrels strong enough to support an elephant."

But sales fell off.

So the manufacturer and the advertising agent investigated. They found that no one believed that barrels could be strong enough to support an elephant—and that the newspaper's readers were convinced that the advertisement showed a fake picture.

Convictions are more dangerous to truth than lies.
—*F. W. Nietzsche, 1878*
Every man is encompassed by a cloud of comforting convictions which move with him like flies on a summer day.
—*Bertrand Russell, 1928*

The Empty Column

WILLIAM J. WISWESSER

Many years ago a Roman civil engineer, who was a high official in Alexandria, was approached by a young Arabian mathematician with an idea which the Arabian believed would be of much value to the Roman Government in their road-building, navigating, tax-collecting, and census-taking activities. As the Arabian explained in his manuscript, he had discovered a new type of notation for number writing, which was inspired from some Hindu inscriptions.

The Roman official presumably studied this manuscript very carefully for several hours, and then wrote the following reply:

Your courier brought your proposal at a time when my duties

were light; so fortunately I have had the opportunity to study it carefully, and am glad to be able to submit these detailed comments.

Your new notation may have a number of merits, as you claim, but it is doubtful whether it ever would be of any practical value to the Roman Empire. Even if authorized by the Emperor himself, as a proposal of this magnitude would have to be, it would be vigorously opposed by the populace, principally because those who had to use it would not sympathize with your radical ideas. Our scribes complain loudly that they have too many letters in the Roman Alphabet as it is, and now you propose these ten additional symbols of your number system, namely

1,2,3,4,5,6,7,8,9, and your 0.

It is clear that your 1–mark has the same meaning as our mark–1, but since this mark–1 already is a well-established character, why is there any need for yours?

Then you explain that last circle–mark like our letter 0, as representing "an empty column," or meaning nothing. If it means nothing, what is the purpose of writing it? I cannot see that it is serving any useful purpose; but to make sure, I asked my assistant to read this section, and he drew the same conclusion.

You say that the number 01 means the same as just 1. This is an intolerable ambiguity and could not be permitted in any legal Roman Documents. Your notation has other ambiguities which seem even worse: You explain that the 1–mark means ONE, yet on the very same page you show it to mean TEN in 10, and one HUNDRED in your 100. If my official duties had not been light while reading this, I would have stopped here; you must realize that examiners will not pay much attention to material containing such obvious errors.

Further on, you claim that your system of numeration is much simpler than with Roman Numerals. I regret to advise that I have examined this point very carefully and must conclude otherwise. For example, counting up to FIVE, you require *five* new symbols whereas we Romans accomplish this with just two old ones, the mark–I and mark–V. At first sight the combination IV (meaning ONE before FIVE) for four may seem less direct than the old IIII, but note that this alert representation involves LESS EFFORT, and that gain is the conquering principle of the Empire.

Counting up to twenty (the commonest counting range among the populace), you require *ten* symbols whereas we now need but three: the I, V, and X. Note particularly the pictorial suggestiveness of the V as *half* of the X. Moreover, it is pictorially evident that XX means ten-and-ten and this seems much preferred over your 20. These pictorial associations are very important to the lower classes, for as the African says, "One picture tell thousand words."

You claim that your numbers as a whole are briefer than the Roman Numerals, but this is not made evident in your proofs. Even if true, it is doubtful that this would mean much to the welfare of the Empire, since numbers account for only a small fraction of the written records; and in any case, there are plenty of slaves with plenty of time to do this work.

When you attempt to show that you can manipulate these numbers much more readily than Roman Numerals, your explanations are particularly bad and obscure. For example, you show in one addition that 2 and 3 equal 5, yet in the case which you write as:

$$
\begin{array}{r}
79 \\
\& \ 16 \\
\hline
95
\end{array}
$$

this indicates that 9 and 6 equal 5. How can this be? While that is not clear, it is evident that the other part is in error, for we know that 7 and 1 equal 8, not 9.

Your so-called "multiplying and dividing" tables also require much more explanation, and possibly correction of errors. I can see that your "Nine Times" Table gives sets which add up to nine, namely

18 27 36 45 54 63 72 81 and 90,

but I see no such useful correlation in the "Seven Times" table, for example. Since we have SEVEN, not nine, days in the Roman Week, it seems far more important to have a system that gives more sensible combinations in this "Seven Times" Table.

All in all, I would advise you to forget this overly ambitious proposal, return to your sand piles, and leave the number reckoning to the official Census Takers and Tax Collectors. I am sure that that they give these matters a great deal more thought than you or I can.

What is valuable is not new, and what is new is not valuable.
>   —Lord Brougham, c. 1839
There is no new thing under the sun.
>   —Ecclesiastes 1:19
What is new is opposed, because most are unwilling to be taught.
>   —Samuel Johnson, 1750
We must view with profound respect the infinite capacity of the
human mind to resist the introduction of useful knowledge.
>   —T. R. Lounsbury, c. 1910
You can't teach an old dog new tricks.
Why change what we have been doing? It's still working OK.
You're years ahead of your time.
It's too radical a change.
Good thought, but impractical.
For eight years I talked about that new idea to all the intelligent
persons whom I could get to listen to me, and for eight years
all my progress was from a blank stare to a broad smile. . . .
And now all the young people study that idea in school as a
part of the new mathematics.

The Differences in Two
Strains of Corn

EDGAR ANDERSON

One of our leading authorities was concerned with two related
strains of corn, one with a higher average row number than the
other. The plants also looked somewhat different and the leaves

looked wider; so he set out to get exact information on this point. He took the leaf above the ear, found its midpoint, and measured the diameter there. He did this for fifty plants of each strain, calculated their averages, and determined mathematically the chances that such an average difference might have come about just anyhow and did not represent a really characteristic difference between the sorts. The chances turned out to be pretty high, and so in his published account of the matter, he was careful to state that he had certainly not demonstrated a difference in the leaf, even after all that work.

Now the simple everyday facts about the leaves of the two strains were as follows. The two sets were of quite a different shape. One was broader and rounder at the base with a slight tendency to be wider in the middle, and it was nearly always shorter than the other. One could easily demonstrate the differences in the two sorts just by stripping off a series of leaves from one set and then a series from the other and laying them down on the earth of the cornfield in two parallel rows. With ten minutes of this kind of work, it was clear that all the leaves of one strain were different from all the leaves of the other. Having seen half a dozen of each kind, one could easily classify at least nineteen out of twenty specimens which had been gathered by an assistant and brought in without a label. One of the results of this basic difference in shape was to make one set a little wider than the other on the average, though the greater width did not necessarily show at the midpoint. With his uncertain reflection of the basic difference in shape, my friend had been struggling in his efforts to get a clear mathematical answer.

We may compare his problem rather exactly to that of separating a pile of oranges from a pile of apples. Apples and oranges being what they are, it might take some fancy mathematics to prove that the two sets of measurements probably came from different kinds of things. If we are willing to study the two fruits before we start out measuring them precisely, then we can see the myriad little differences between apples and oranges, and any normal child can separate the two lots in a moment.

All of this was lost on my friend, not because he did not have a good mind, not because he was not industrious, but simply because he had not learned to look at a corn plant or, for that matter, any other plant. He was a most intelligent person, but he had never been given even the beginnings of training in natural history. I found to my horror that although he had spent his adult life studying corn, he understood almost nothing of its technical architecture. Yet he was one of our very best corn geneticists and a man to whom students came, up until the day of his death, from all over the world.

He had been convinced as a young man that the taxonomic method was old-fogyish, and he would have none of it.

If we are willing to study the two fruits before we start measuring them precisely, then we can see the myriad little differences between apples and oranges, and any normal child can separate them in a moment.

All this was lost on my friend, not because he did not have a good mind, not because he was not industrious, but simply because he had not learned to look at a corn plant, or for that matter, any other plant.

He had been convinced as a young man that the . . . method was old-fogyish and he would have none of it.

Who is so blind as he who will not see?

—*John Ray, 1670*

A man can be an expert in one part of a subject, yet ignorant and blind in another part.

There is an art to observing well.

An expert can disdain and scorn information offered contrary to the usual manner in which he acquires his information.

Mathematics contains no rules complete enough to tell precisely to what observations mathematics should be applied.

The Six Blind Men of Nepal

EDMUND C. BERKELEY

Once upon a time in the highlands of Nepal, there lived six blind men who had heard many conflicting stories about a great beast called the elephant. And this led to many heated arguments among them.

So they agreed they would go down to the jungle in the low-lands of Nepal, and investigate the elephant at first hand. They would observe for themselves. With the help of a rather casual and careless guide who could see, they found in the jungle a sleeping elephant, and they touched him for a minute or two—until the elephant waked up and trumpeted, whereupon they all fled.

Later, the six blind men, having returned to the highlands of Nepal, gathered together once more, and sought to fit their observations together. However, this resulted in even more arguments than before—for the six reports of the six blind men were these:

The elephant is like a tree trunk (this blind man felt the elephant's leg).
The elephant is like string (this one felt the tail).
The elephant is like paper (this one felt the ear).
The elephant is like a bone (this one felt the tusk).
The elephant is like a pig (this one felt the body).
The elephant is like a snake (this one felt the elephant's trunk).

At last after many days of heated discussion, the six blind men did agree unanimously on six propositions:

(1) By straining their imagination, they could imagine an animal that had two, or perhaps three, of these properties;

(2) But they could not possibly conceive of an animal that had all six of these properties;

(3) Therefore, as a beast, the elephant was impossible;

(4) Certainly, it was as legendary as the unicorn or the griffin;

(5) The trumpeting they had all heard was undoubtedly a jungle illusion, that happened from time to time in the jungles of the lowlands of Nepal;

(6) Henceforth, they would forbid all discussion of the elephant—to avoid the arguments, the friction, and the waste of time.

Truth is hidden at the bottom of a well.

> —*Democritus, c. 400* B.C.

Truth often hides in an ugly pool.

> —*Chinese proverb*

Truth lurks in deep hiding and is wrapped in mystery.

> —*Seneca,* A.D. *64*

There are stranger things in reality than can be found in romances.

> —*T. C. Haliburton, 1843*

At times truth may not seem probable.

> —*Boileau, 1674*

There are more things in heaven and earth, Horatio, than are dreamt of in your philosophy.

> —*Shakespeare, 1601*

Falsehood is so near to truth that a wise man would do well not to trust himself on such a narrow edge.

> —*Cicero, c. 45* B.C.

Truth always lags behind falsehood, limping along on the arm of time.

> —*Baltasar Gracian, 1647*

The most mischievous liars are those who keep sliding on the very verge of truth.

> —*J. C. and A. W. Hare, 1827*

The most curious aspect of truth seems to be that nobody will believe it. We can swallow any number of falsehoods and fancies but not the truth.

> —*J. S. Strange, 1943*

Truth is stranger than fiction.

The world is more complicated than most of our theories make it out to be.

The Sighting of a Whale

EDMUND C. BERKELEY

Once upon a time a precocious young fox named Redmond Reynard (Reddy for short) sighted a large whale in the ocean some distance off from the large rocky promontory where he and his family lived. Excitedly, he called his mother and pointed it out to her.

That afternoon at tea-time Mrs. Fox started telling several lady fox guests about the whale which she and Reddy had seen that morning.

Mrs. Fox mentioned that the whale was about a mile away. At the first possible opening in the conversation, Reddy said, politely and softly, "No, mother, the whale was nearer; it was about three-quarters of a mile away."

A moment later, Mrs. Fox remarked that they had seen the whale about eleven o'clock. Reddy promptly said, "No, mother, it was about twenty minutes to eleven."

A little later his mother mentioned that they had watched the whale for about five minutes. "No mother," said Reddy, "we watched it for nine minutes. I timed it."

When the lady fox guests had gone, Mrs. Fox reprimanded Reddy, and said to him, "You mustn't correct me that way. It is rude, impolite, and not necessary. Now, Reddy, you love to take notes. Put down what I have just told you so that you will remember."

Reddy wrote something down in his notebook.

Mrs. Fox said, "Show me what you have written."

Reddy showed her, "Truth is not necessary."

Mrs. Fox laughed. Then she said, "No, Reddy, that's not it. Cross that out and write 'Accuracy is not always essential.'"

"Truth is not necessary."

Accuracy is not always essential.

An hair's breadth fixed by a divine finger, shall prove as effectual a
separation from danger as a mile's distance.
—*Thomas Fuller, 1655*

He was very near being a poet—but a miss is as good as a mile, and
he always fell short of the distance.
—*Walter Scott, 1825*

With any not insupportable approximation, we must be patient.

The Stars and the Young Rabbit

EDMUND C. BERKELEY

The Young Rabbit and the Old Rabbit, who was his teacher, were
lying in thick green grass near their burrow, looking at more than
a hundred stars in the night sky. They were chewing cabbage
leaves in an interlude between lessons.

Young Rabbit: Why are there stars in the night sky?

Old Rabbit: The stars are in the sky both in the nighttime and
the daytime, but in the daytime the sky is so bright that you can't
see the stars.

Young Rabbit: Oh, that's strange. Why?

Old Rabbit: It can be proved but I don't remember the proof.

Young Rabbit: Oh! Then why should I believe what you say?

Old Rabbit: You don't have to believe it.

Young Rabbit: Oh, but why don't I have to believe it since you
are a Teacher Rabbit, and you've said it?

Old Rabbit: Because Teacher Rabbits say many kinds of truth.
Some truths make an enormous difference to young rabbits—such
as that foxes mean danger—and other truths make very little dif-

ference to young rabbits—such as that the stars do actually shine in the daytime.

Young Rabbit: (in a doubtful tone, as if he were trying to understand but didn't) Oh!

Old Rabbit: If a young rabbit does not believe the important truths, he dies soon and miserably. If a young rabbit does believe the important truths, he has a chance to live a long and happy life. But it's not guaranteed.

Young Rabbit: Oh, tell me quickly all the important truths. Then as soon as I know them all, I can run away from the schoolroom and play.

Old Rabbit: No rabbit anywhere knows enough so that he can say about a collection of statements: "These and only these are the important statements." Every collection of important truths made by any rabbit has to be tagged with question marks—with a label that reads "tentative."

Young Rabbit: That's very troublesome. Why haven't the Teacher Rabbits discovered all the important truths?

Old Rabbit: (thoughtfully) There are many reasons. One of the main reasons is that no matter how much any rabbit learns, there is always more to learn.

Young Rabbit: Why?

Old Rabbit: (looking squarely at the Young Rabbit and smiling at him) Because any rabbit, especially a young rabbit, can always ask again "Why?" Rabbits are always curious, always inquisitive.

Young Rabbit: Why?

The first and simplest emotion which we discover in the human mind is curiosity.

    —*Edmund Burke, 1756*

Talk to him of Jacob's ladder and he would ask the number of steps.

    —*D. Jerrold, 1850*

God fashioned hell for the inquisitive.

    —*St. Augustine,* A.D. 397

Curiosity is endless, restless, and useless.

—*Thomas Fuller, 1732*

Wonder is the only beginning of philosophy.

—*Plato, c. 390 B.C.*

Wonders will never cease.

—*H. B. Dudley, 1776*

Any river is huge if it is the greatest a man has seen.

—*Lucretius, c. 45 B.C.*

Wonder is the daughter of ignorance.

—*Thomas Fuller, 1732*

The Ocean of Truth

SIR ISAAC NEWTON

I do not know what I may appear to the world, but to myself I seem to have been only like a boy playing on the sea-shore, and diverting myself in now and then finding a smoother pebble or a prettier shell than ordinary, whilst the great ocean of truth lay all undiscovered before me.

A man is but what he knoweth.

—*Francis Bacon, 1626*

Man approaches the unattainable truth through a succession of errors.

—*Aldous Huxley*

What man knows is not to be compared with what he does not know.

—*Chuang-Tsze, c. 400 B.C.*

Part VI

ON
COMMON
SENSE

THE·LARK AND ·HER YOUNG·ONES.

The Lark and Her Young Ones

AESOP

In the spring a Lark made her nest in a field full of young green wheat, and in a few weeks the young ones had almost grown to full strength. When she flew off to forage for them, she charged them strictly to gather what news they could, and report to her when she came back.

One day on her return, they told her that the owner of the field had been there, and said aloud, "The time has come when I must ask my neighbors to help me with the harvest." And they said to her, "Mother, where shall we flee so as to be safe?"

The mother Lark said, "There's no real danger yet."

When she returned the next day, they told her the owner had been there once more and said, "This field is ripe. I must get my friends to help me harvest it."

The mother Lark said, "There's no danger in that either."

Upon the third day, the young ones told their mother that the owner had been there again, and had noticed that some of his ears of wheat were shedding their grain on the ground, and he had said, "I must come tomorrow with my hired hands, and we will reap this field ourselves."

When the mother Lark heard this report, she said to her young ones, "Now there is danger, and we must leave today—for the owner is no longer trusting to his neighbors or his friends, but he is going to reap the field himself with his own laborers."

He that would be sure to have his business well done, must either
  do it himself or see to the doing of it.
                                                    —*Sir Roger L'Estrange*
One's own hand is the surest and promptest help.
                                                    —*La Fontaine, 1678*

If you'd have it done, go: if not, send.

—*Benjamin Franklin, 1743*

If you want a thing well done, do it yourself.

—*Vincent Lean, 1902*

The Bear and the Young Dog

EDMUND C. BERKELEY

Once there was a Bear who was a good carpenter. The Lion hired him to build a new Lion house, because as he said to the Bear, the Lioness was very tired of living in an old-fashioned cave, with no chimney for the smoke, cold drafts, and all that nuisance, and she had been talking to him about it morning and night for days.

So the Bear agreed, and set to work.

One day the Bear was working hard at shaping a roof beam, and he called to his helper, a Young Dog, and said to him: "Look in my toolbox over there and bring me my plane."

The Young Dog came back in a moment and said, "Sir, it isn't there."

The Bear growled. Then he said, "That's ridiculous—to say 'It isn't there.' You can't prove that. All you can truthfully say is 'I didn't find it.' Now go back there and look harder."

In a moment the Young Dog returned, his tail between his legs, bringing the plane.

"It isn't there" is an interpretation; "I did not find it" is a fact. Interpretations must never be confused with facts.

In order to report correctly on the real world, we need a profound respect for it.

The Bear and the Young Calf

EDMUND C. BERKELEY

The Bear was working on a Lion house for the Lions who wanted to move out of their old-fashioned, drafty cave.

One day, his usual helper, the Young Dog, was sick, and so a friend, a Young Calf, replaced him as the Bear's helper.

The Bear said, "See all those shingles? Move them carefully from that heap where they were dropped when they were delivered, to the foot of the ladder where I can carry them up with me as I shingle the roof."

The Bear then took half a dozen shingles under his arm, put a handful of roof-nails in his mouth, and carrying his hammer, climbed up the ladder to the roof, and nailed the shingles in the right places.

As he came down the ladder, he noticed the Young Calf carrying one shingle at a time from the heap to the foot of the ladder.

The Bear growled. "By Gemini," he cried out, "why are you carrying those shingles just one at a time?"

The Calf said, "You told me to carry them carefully. You did not say not to carry them one at a time."

The Bear growled again. "Carefully, yes, of course, carefully," he said, "but that doesn't mean one at a time. How can I tell you not to do something if I can't imagine what you will do? Take the shingles in reasonable loads, and carry them carefully."

Why are you carrying those shingles just one at a time?
How can I tell you not to do something if I can't imagine what you will do?

A fool has no common sense and even less judgment.
Untrained helpers will make all the mistakes in the book—plus
    some entirely new ones.
If a new worker understands the words of his supervisor without
    a concrete demonstration of what is intended, a miracle has
    happened.

The Bear and the Young Beaver

EDMUND C. BERKELEY

The Bear was still working as a carpenter on a Lion house for the
Lions, who wanted to move out of their old cave.

One day an eager young animal, a Young Beaver, was his helper.

The Bear was putting in panes of glass in the new Lion house.
The Young Beaver was helping with a great deal of energy; and
some of the time, while waiting for instructions, was playing with
a ball in his pocket. All of a sudden the ball slipped out of his
grasp and broke one of the panes of glass.

The Young Beaver went at once to the Bear, and explained the
accident, and said he was sorry.

The Bear said, "I am glad you're sorry, but being sorry doesn't
mend the pane of glass. Go down to the hardware store, buy a
pane of glass, bring it back, and put it in."

So the Young Beaver took out the remaining broken glass, measured the space, wrote down the dimensions, went to the hardware
store, bought a pane of glass, came back, and started to put it in.

But the glass did not fit. He measured the space again. He looked
at the dimensions he had written down. What he had written
down was wrong.

He explained to the Bear. The Bear said, "I am glad you are sorry you measured wrong, but that does not repair the pane of glass. Try again."

So the Young Beaver measured the space again very carefully, brought back another pane of glass, and put it in. It fitted. But as he was reaching for the glazier's points to fasten it in, his elbow hit the pane, and it fell out, and broke.

Again he explained to the Bear. The Bear said, "I am glad you are sorry that you knocked it out and it broke, but that does not repair the pane of glass. Try again."

So the Young Beaver went down to the store for a third time, bought a third pane of glass and brought it back. With the greatest care he fitted it into the space, and immediately tacked it in with glazier's points. Then he fastened the pane in with putty.

The Bear, noticing that the task was now complete, said to the Young Beaver, "I am glad you succeeded. Now do this for me. . . ."

In success is the crown of perfect glory.

—*Pindar, c. 476* B.C.

Nothing succeeds like success.

—*Alexandre Dumas, 1854*

Genius is an infinite capacity for taking pains.

—*Jane Ellice Hopkins, 1870*

Sorrow makes us wise.

—*Tennyson, 1850*

Better to be careful than to be sorry.

Less eagerness and more carefulness is often a better strategy.

THE·WASPS AND THE·HONEY·POT·

The Wasps and the Honey Pot

AESOP AND SIR ROGER L'ESTRANGE

There was a whole swarm of wasps that discovered an overturned honey pot. There they cloyed and fettered themselves, till there was no getting away again; which brought them to understand in the end that they had paid too dear for their sweetmeats.

Easy is the descent to Avernus.

—*Vergil*, 19 B.C.

Wide is the gate and broad is the way that leadeth to destruction.

—*St. Matthew*

. . . the primrose way to the everlasting bonfire.

—*Shakespeare*, 1606

The gates of hell are open night and day,
Smooth the descent and easy is the way.

—*John Dryden*, 1697

The Six-Day War and the Gulf of Dong

EDMUND C. BERKELEY

Once there was a wise and clever and beautiful queen whose name was Queen Kernizahde, who could tell excellent stories. And one evening her husband, King Nasheednezzar, said to her: "My dear, I have had a long and difficult day in the Court Room—you know, decisions, decisions, decisions. I am too tired to read, or to look at pictures, or to play games. I would like to lie here on this couch and hold your hand, my dear, while you sit by me and tell me an interesting and puzzling and baffling story."

The Queen, with a sweet and lovely smile, patted the King, her husband, and said, "My Lord, I hear and obey." And this was the story that she told.

Once upon a time there existed two countries, Alphadarea and Betakeepia. Alphadarea was a big country with 90 million people and three presidents, and Betakeepia was a small country with 2 million people, and one prime minister. For many years there had been ill feeling between these two countries—and two prior wars, both of which Alphadarea had lost.

Finally, a day came when the three presidents of Alphadarea declared that the country of Betakeepia had no right to exist. They demanded that certain international peace-keeping forces along a prior armistice line should be at once removed. They were removed the next day by the secretary-general who acted for all the countries of the world. Whereupon the great army of Alphadarea at once moved into the vacant, previously neutral territory, which had been part of Alphadarea before the end of the second war eight years earlier.

The armies of Alphadarea also occupied a fortress that was located at the mouth of the Gulf of Dong, a long gulf with a narrow strait for entrance, called Ding Dong Strait, three miles wide. Betakeepia had a seaport on the Gulf of Dong, which gave her access to a second ocean.

During the next ten days the soldiers of Alphadarea allowed the ships of all countries to pass through Ding Dong Strait—but they shot at and thereby stopped any ships of Betakeepia from passing through the strait in either direction. The government of Betakeepia knew that passage of their ships through Ding Dong Strait was absolutely vital to their interests.

Betakeepia appealed to all the other countries in the world to request, order, and compel Alphadarea to allow the ships of Betakeepia to pass through Ding Dong Strait—as they had been doing for the previous eight years.

The other countries made requests using nice firm diplomatic words—but the three presidents of Alphadarea said loudly and clearly, "No."

The intermittent shelling of a northern zone of Betakeepia, which had continued for years from an adjacent mountainous region of Alphadarea, grew in intensity. The great armies of Alphadarea now touched all the boundaries of Betakeepia. The three presidents of Alphadarea and all the newspapers of Alphadarea and all their ambassadors to other countries declared that the Alphadareans were going to occupy all of Betakeepia, that their war was a holy war, that they would lay waste to and ravage all of Betakeepia, and that Betakeepia would cease to exist as a country.

The Betakeepians appealed to all the countries of the world to protect them from what the Alphadareans said they were going to do. The other countries however explained to the Betakeepians that probably the Alphadareans were just talking in a loud voice and did not mean what they were saying, and that in any case if they did, they would slap the Alphadareans on their wrists.

The prime minster and the government of Betakeepia waited for ten days to find out what the other countries of the world were going to do about access through Ding Dong Strait (it turned out to be nothing), and to listen to what the Alphadareans said they were going to do (which was clearly dangerous), and to estimate what the other countries of the world would do about the Alphadarean threats (that turned out to be nothing).

Then early on the morning of the 11th day of waiting, the Betakeepian army attacked in force.

Less than four days later, the armies of Alphadarea had been beaten, had disintegrated, and had fled, to distant parts of Alphadarea. The army of Betakeepia had occupied the whole of the formerly neutral territory, and much additional territory of Alphadarea, to the south, to the west, and to the north, Particularly, the Betakeepian army had occupied the mountainous border region to the north from which Betakeepia had been bombarded for many years, and also the Ding Dong Fortress at the mouth of the Gulf of Dong, from which Betakeepian ships had been shelled.

Over 30,000 soldiers of Alphadarea were dead; less than 1000 soldiers of Betakeepia were dead.

As soon as the tide of battle became clear, that the Betakeepians were winning a colossal victory, the other countries of the world jumped into action. They set to work to organize and compel a ceasefire. The ceasefire took effect on the sixth day following the attack, just in time to prevent the three presidents of Alphadarea from losing their jobs.

And after that time, the situation, strange to say, just stayed in the new arrangement—with no peace treaty, no agreements, no settlements—from day to day, and from month to month, and from year to year.

"And that is the end of my story," the Queen said.

King Nasheednezzar: My dear, that is one of the strangest stories I ever heard. I don't think it could possibly happen. It is not believable.

Queen Kernizahde: But it did happen, my Lord.

King: Then it did not happen in our world.

Queen: There you are right, my Lord. It happened in a different world from ours.

King: On what basis did the three presidents of Alphadarea estimate that they could win?

Queen: There were a number of reasons, all of which of course proved false. They thought they had enough people, soldiers, friends, allies, arms, sources of aid, and knowledge. They thought they had enough courage; they were sure they had enough hatred of the Betakeepians. They thought they had promised their soldiers enough incentives, looting, raping, and killing. And because they had three presidents, each did not dare to seem less than really brave to the other two.

King: What a huge mistake the Alphadarean leaders made! Did they learn as a result?

Queen: I don't think so. Usually, huge mistakes result in teachable moments. But whether or not a teachable moment resulted for Alphadarea is hard to say. Probably the ceasefire came much too soon for the necessary historical lessons to have been learned by Alphadarea.

King: How did you find out that puzzling and baffling story?

Queen: A traveler from that world told it to me. My Lord, I did not believe it at first either; but he showed me lots of evidence.

King: Hm!

Whom God wishes to destroy, he first makes mad.
> —*Euripides, c. 425* B:C.

Those whom God would ruin, he first deprives of reason.
> —*Boswell, 1783*

Whom the gods intend to make miserable, they first lead into error.
> —*Sophocles, c. 441* B.C.

We learn not in school but in life.
> —*Seneca,* A.D. *64*

In almost everything experience is more valuable than precept.
> —*Quintilian,* A.D. *80*

Experience is the mistress of knaves as well as of fools.
> —*Sir Roger L'Estrange, 1692*

Never pursue a difficult enterprise with three co-equal leaders.

The Deceived Eagle

JAMES NORTHCOTE

An Eagle soaring aloft saw beneath him what he fancied to be a fine fat hare sleeping on a bank in the sun; and, being rather sharp set in his appetite, he descended rapidly from his towering height, and without performing the ceremony of making a minute examination of his intended prey, boldly darted upon his victim carrying it away triumphantly in his talons. But he had not flown to any great height before he discovered the fatal error committed, on feeling his throat seized by the deadly grip, not of a Hare, but of an enraged Wild Cat, the mistaken object of his rapacity. And thus he fell to the ground and expired on the spot.

Application

There is nothing that looks sillier than a crafty knave, outwitted and beaten at his own game, and by his own weapons. Neither is it an object of pity, when we witness the rapacious and bloodthirsty falling into disgrace and ruin by their own selfish and cruel machinations.

It is costly wisdom that is bought by experience.
—*Roger Ascham, c. 1565*
The things which hurt, instruct.
—*Benjamin Franklin, 1744*

Missile Alarm from Grunelandt

EDMUND C. BERKELEY

On another occasion, King Nasheednezzar said to his wise and beautiful Queen Kernizahde: "My dear, that was an interesting, puzzling, and baffling story that you told me the other evening. I am weary again this evening—those Royal Court problems take effort to solve. Do tell me another story." And he stretched out on the couch.

The Queen patted her King; and sitting down in a chair beside the couch, she said with a sweet smile, because she thoroughly enjoyed telling stories and loved to be asked to tell them, "My Lord, I hear and obey." And this was the story she told.

Once upon a time there were two very large and strong countries called Bazunia and Vossnia. There were many great, important, and powerful leaders in Bazunia, a whole class of them in fact, who carefully cultivated an enormous fear of Vossnia. Over and over again these important and powerful Bazunian leaders would say to their fellow countrymen, "You can't trust the Vossnians." And in Vossnia there was a group of great, important, and powerful leaders, a whole class of them in fact, who pointed out what dangerous military activities the Bazunians were carrying on, and how Vossnia had to be militarily strong to counteract them.

The Bazunian leaders persuaded their countrymen to vote to give them enormous sums of money to construct something called a Ballistic Missile Early Warning System; and one of its stations was installed in a land called Grunelandt far to the north of Bazunia.

Now, of course, ballistic missiles loaded with nuclear explosives can fly any kind of a path all around a spherical world, and they do not have to fly over northern regions. And even a small number of nuclear explosives from ballistic missiles can wipe out cities, and produce vast firestorms, and their use on any kind of broad scale implied millions of people dead for both Bazunia and Vossnia. There was no good reason for the Bazunians to believe that the Vossnians would fly their ballistic missiles over the region north of Bazunia instead of some other way.

But this kind of reasoning had no influence on the leaders of Bazunia who wanted the money for building BMEWS. Nor did it have influence on their countrymen, who were always busy, trying to make money in other ways—in fact often too busy to think clearly.

So the Ballistic Missile Early Warning System was bought and installed, for billions of Bazunian francs.

Now one day, the station of the Ballistic Missile Early Warning System at Laithu, in Grunelandt, which had been finished, ". . . picked up signals which were analyzed by the computers there as a flight of missiles coming up over the horizon from Vossnia and heading in the direction of Bazunia. What was called the 'famous red telephone' rang at Bazunian Air Force Command headquarters in the middle of Bazunia at a place called Skar. All over the world at outlying bases of Bazunia, air crews ran to their planes. Someone at Skar headquarters signalled Laithu for confirmation. There was no answer. . . ."

It happened at just this time that three Bazunian businessmen

leaders were touring the Bazunian Defense Command headquarters at Rardo, hundreds of miles away from Skar. They were
three presidents of three great businesses; the name of one was
Smith. The guide showed the three executives the equipment designed to detect the presence of missiles, and pointed out a lighted
panel with a series of numbers running from one through five.

"As I recall it," President Smith said later, "we were told if No.
1 flashed, it meant only routine objects were in the air. If No. 2
flashed, it meant a few more unidentified objects, but nothing
suspicious. If No. 5 flashed, it was highly probable that objects in
a raid were moving toward Bazunia. As we watched the screen, the
number changed from 1 to 2, then there was a pause, then it
changed to 3, then the number changed to 4. When the number
rose to 4 key generals came running from their offices. Then the
number rose to 5. The other two men and I were escorted from
the main room into another office; we did not know what happened in the great defense staff room after we left. We were
stunned. We waited through twenty minutes of absolute terror.
We talked. Our first thoughts were of our families; they weren't
with us and we could not reach them. It was a rather hopeless
feeling. But then you realize there's very little you can do if a
missile attack is on the way."

At the central defense headquarters of Rardo at that time, Air
Marshal Mont, deputy commander-in-chief was in command, in
the absence of Air Force General Terr, away on inspection. Radar
information made it appear that long-range missiles had been
launched against Bazunia, and the current range was 2200 miles.

But General Mont "refused to be panicked." He lacked other
confirming evidence: (1) he knew that I. Shchev, the Vossnian
premier, was actually in Bazunia that day on his way to a meeting
of countries of the whole world; (2) none of the other radar warning lines, the Distant Early Warning Line, the Rentian Line, or
the Pinetree Line, reported any strange echoes; (3) and finally the
equipment that predicts areas of impact of missiles displayed no
areas of impact at all.

Finally, the information came in from Laithu that the radar
pulses were taking 75 seconds to echo, whereas from missiles they
would echo in one-eighth of a second.

In a moment General Mont decided the report of missiles arriving from Vossnia was highly questionable. He telephoned the

commander at Laithu, and was told that the Ballistic Missile Early Warning System "was not operating properly."

By the time that Laithu had discovered the error, that they "had picked up not a squadron of rockets, but a large earth satellite—called the moon," they were prevented from passing on the correction to headquarters at Skar "because an iceberg had cut their submarine cable link."

The Ballistic Missile Early Warning System had reported a range of 2200 miles, because "it had divided 3000 miles into the distance to the moon, and had reported the distance left over, 2200, as the range."

Of course, the Ballistic Missile Early Warning System was promptly "taught" to disregard radar echoes from the moon.

But what would have happened if General Mont, the Bazunian general who happened to have the responsibility at that moment, had accepted the report "missiles on their way from Vossnia" and ordered retaliation?

King Nasheednezzar: That's a very strange story: interesting, puzzling, baffling. And you finish it with a question to me! It is hardly believable. Is it a real story?

Queen Kernizahde: Yes, it is a real story, in another world, of course, my Lord. Are you interested in trying to answer the question?

King: Yes. My answer is that if that General had accepted that report and ordered retaliation, there would have been a colossal disaster, with millions of people dead, maybe even hundreds of millions dead—and all on account of an accident, an error from machines and human beings operating in a system together which was too complicated for their little minds and little emotions. Those Bazunians and Vossnians must be crazy to play that kind of game. They are crazy, aren't they?

Queen: Yes, they are crazy, and not only crazy but dangerous. But they have a wonderful system for convincing each other that they are normal and full of common sense: each person talks to everyone else around him, and they compare what they all say and call the summation "public opinion," and if they all say and believe the same things, then they conclude that they are all normal and not crazy.

King: By the gods of Babyria and Assylon, I am glad we don't decide things that way!

There were a great many important and powerful leaders in Bazunia who carefully cultivated an enormous fear of Vossnia. Over and over again these leaders would say to their fellow countrymen, "You can't trust the Vossnians." And in Vossnia there were a great many important and powerful leaders who pointed out what dangerous military activities the Bazunians were carrying on and how Vossnia had to be militarily strong to counteract them.

But this sensible kind of reasoning had no influence on the common people who were always busy and distracted—in fact, often too busy and distracted to think clearly.

There would have been a colossal disaster, with millions of people dead, all on account of an accident, an error, from machines and people operating in a system together which was too complicated for their little minds and little emotions.

Those people must be crazy to play that kind of game; they are crazy, aren't they?—Yes, they are crazy, and not only crazy but dangerous. But they have a wonderful system for convincing each other that they are normal and full of common sense: each person talks to everyone else around him, and they compare what they all say and call the summation "public opinion"; and if they all say and believe the same things, then they conclude that they are all normal and not crazy.

The most fear the world's opinion, more than God's displeasure.
—*Sir Thomas Overbury,* 1613
That is true which all men say.
—*John Ray,* 1678

Popular opinion is the greatest lie in the world.
> —*Thomas Fuller, 1732*

Public opinion works by contagion, and swiftly seizes a great number of men.
> —*Leo Tolstoy, 1893*

The National Security of Adularia

EDMUND C. BERKELEY

Once upon a time, on a fine spring evening, King Nasheednezzar said to his wise and beautiful Queen Kernizahde, "My dear, your stories are always interesting, puzzling, and baffling, and give me much relaxation from the tiring affairs of my royal day. Please tell me another story."

The Queen smiled, because she loved to tell stories, and was flattered to be asked, and she said, "My Lord, I hear and obey," and this was the story she told.

Once upon a time there was a very large and very strong country called Adularia. In this country there were two groups of people. One group was the little people, who were not very wealthy but very numerous; and they were given to adulation of leaders. The other group was the important people, who were few in number, and were all either wealthy or distinguished, and who were considered to be the leaders by the little people; and they also were given to adulation of the top important person, who was called the "president."

In fact, no matter who among the important people was elected to be president, after he was elected, he was considered to be so superior to everybody else, no one else ever compelled him or forced him to answer a question. For whenever he said, "I can't answer that question on grounds of national security," that was the end of the question.

And there was once a man in that country whose name was

Maximilianson-Louiscendent. He dreamed of being an emperor like Maximilian or a king like the Louis's of France. He would think of the motto of King Louis XIV, the Great Monarch, "L'état, c'est moi." "The state, that's me." He would dream of the adulation he would receive as the president of Adularia; and he resolved that nothing, but nothing, would stand in his way. He was very ambitious and a shrewd, smart politician. His ten-syllable name was much too long to suit him, and so he changed it to Maxon.

Being very industrious, persevering, and clever, Maxon studied the ins and outs of the system of Adularia and the government of Adularia. He learned all the ways of doing things: the aboveboard ways, the underhand ways, and the pretend ways, in the style of what was called "public relations," in which you say one thing and do something else. He became a very astute and cunning expert in politics. And particularly he learned how to use beautiful phrases with vague meanings like the magic phrase "national security."

He approached the important leaders of Adularia, and he said to them, "I have become an expert at all levels, bar none, in the system and the government of Adularia. I can help you a great deal if I become president." And he persuaded the important people to seek to arrange his election as president of Adularia. This they agreed to do, in return for his promises to reward them, spoken and unspoken, according to the great operating principle of politics in Adularia, "You scratch my back and I will scratch yours," which is also known in that country as the principle of division of labor, that is to say, political labor.

Before Maxon was elected president for the first time, the leading opposition candidate (who was the brother of a previously assassinated, but much praised president of Adularia) was also assassinated. This happened just at the moment when he won the opposing party's primary election in the largest of the states of Adularia. His death was most unfortunate. But it must be admitted that this was extremely timely and convenient for Maxon, and it essentially guaranteed that the presidential election would be won by Maxon.

Candidate Maxon made speeches. To all the people he said, "If you elect me, I will make sure that there is a great increase in national security." To the important people he said, "I will make sure that the rich and powerful get richer and more powerful." To the little people he said, "I will make sure that the central government shares its revenue with the cities and the states." Candidate Maxon was elected, and became president.

Then at last he started to put into effect the proposition known as Maxon's First Law: "The national security of Adularia is identical with the interests of President Maxon." But he never did tell anybody about this proposition; he kept it secret. For a long time only his actions revealed the existence of Maxon's First Law.

During the first four years of his presidency, Maxon set out to advance and promote "national security." He emphasized that newspapers should not print what was called "classified information," information that any member or employee of the government had decided should be secret and so they had marked it (i.e., "classified" it) as secret on account of "national security."

A few newspapers did publish such information, showing that parts of the government were corrupt. Also, a man named Carlsberg, a renegade from among the important people, gave classified information to the newspapers. Maxon called this person and the newspapers "traitors to the national security of Adularia." The Department of Justice of Adularia, which a few people unkindly called the Department of Injustice, started legal suits against these "traitors," and these caused the defendants to incur enormous expenses in adulars, the currency of Adularia.

At last after four years as president, Maxon was up for reelection. He talked to the important people who were his friends and supporters, and who had received favors from him during the four years—raises in the price of milk, advance knowledge of large foreign grain sales, and so on, and so on. He received secretly many large contributions to his reelection campaign.

Then one day about five months before the date of election, a most unpleasant surprise occurred for President Maxon. Five men were discovered and arrested at two o'clock in the morning burglarizing the national headquarters office of the opposing political party in the Milkgate Building in the capital city of Adularia. These men were arrested with electronic listening devices and burglars' tools. Because of the nosy investigation of a couple of "traitorous" newspaper reporters of one of the opposition newspapers in the capital city, it turned out that some of the men had been on the payroll of Maxon's reelection committee until that very moment. Also, two of the men had had offices in the Gold and Purple House, which was the operational headquarters of President Maxon.

At that moment President Maxon realized that all of this affair had to be hushed up in the interests of national security. So it was called a "prank" instead of a "burglary," and a "caper" instead of a "crime"; and funny stories were spread about it, "boys will be boys, you know." How tragic and how dangerous it would be for the national security if the people of Adularia thought that the president might have had anything to do with this burglary!

Using his great resources and his faithful staff, he arranged for a cover-up operation. Only these seven men would be guilty. Above them would be a line of innocence. He called the event "a bizarre incident." Using as much influence as necessary, all of six different investigations that had started were smothered or delayed. Nothing was to come out or be revealed before election day. And election day came around, and Maxon won a "landside victory" re-election. The opposing candidate carried just one of the 50 states of Adularia.

But after the reelection, most unfortunately, President Maxon was not quite able to control all the crucial details of the Milkgate Crime. A legal trial began soon after the election. A nasty judge who was incorruptible was in charge of it. The "ball of wax," which was really a "waxed ball of string," started to unwax, unwind, and unravel.

First, the nasty judge challenged the statements of many of the witnesses when they said they could not remember crucial facts that everybody ordinarily would have remembered.

Second, one of the seven men who was faced with a long term prison sentence did not believe the promise conveyed to him by a colleague of President Maxon, that he would receive executive clemency and be out of prison before a year was over; and this nasty man decided to tell all he knew.

Worst of all Maxon found he had really offended the important people who had connections with the opposite political party. Nothing that Maxon could think of doing or offering or promising or paying could apparently rectify this mistake. It was too late.

Gradually these "traitors to national security" among the important people organized a real challenge to Maxon's First Law:

"The interests of national security are identical with the interests of President Maxon." For these nasty important people had at last discovered Maxon's First Law, and they felt they could no longer tolerate it.

And so Maxon's whole structure of government centered in him began to crumble. The beautifully painted images of Maxon and his policies began to be shown for the mirages they really were. The definition of national security began to be changed back from "the interests of Maxon and his colleagues" to "the security of the country and people of Adularia." And all the people of Adularia began to be given a new chance not to be fooled—to "have a republic, if they could make it work."

"And that is the end of my story," said the Queen.

The King: My dear, you score again—that is an interesting, puzzling, and baffling story. In fact, it is unbelievable.

Queen: But it is a true story.

King: Not in our world.

Queen: In that other world, my Lord, that we were talking about.

King: Do tell me what happened next.

Queen: My Lord, my knowledge of the events in that other world depends on what travellers to our land have told me—and so far no traveller arriving here has told me what happened next.

King: I see. But why were the people of Adularia so deceived? Why didn't they look behind the images, and the lies, and the cover of "national security"? Why did they fail to use their common sense?

Queen: A few of them did, of course, but not many. My Lord, it is difficult for us in our country to imagine how those people could have been so deceived. But there is a basic reason.

Consider the machines, equipment, and supplies—the technology—for informing people in general about what is going on in the world. That technology becomes more and more expensive, and more and more powerful. Along the road of development and progress of that technology, there is a place where all that technology has become so expensive and so powerful that it is monopolized and controlled by the establishment. When that place along the road is reached, it produces the predictable end of the rights of an ordinary citizen to be informed, to know the truth, to hear conflicting sides to the news and to arguments. In our country we are still very far from that place. But Adularia is much farther along that road of development, and is very near to that place. And in that world where Adularia is, several countries have got to that place on the road and beyond.

King: Oh, by the gods of Babyria and Assylon, we must arrange not to go down that road!

No matter who among the important people was elected to be president, after he was elected, he was considered to be so superior to everybody else that no one ever compelled him or forced him to answer a question.

He learned all the ways of doing things: the aboveboard ways, the underhand ways, and the pretend ways, in the style of what was called "public relations," in which you say one thing and do something else.

All of this affair had to be hushed up in the interests of "national security." So it was called a "prank" instead of a "burglary" and a "caper" instead of a "crime." And funny stories were spread about it, "boys will be boys, you know."

The state has no worse foe than a tyrant.
                                        —*Euripides, c.* 421 B.C.
Rebellion to tyrants is obedience to God.
                                        —*Thomas Jefferson*
Clever tyrants are never punished.
                                        —*Voltaire,* 1743

Doomsday in St. Pierre, Martinique

EDMUND C. BERKELEY

Once upon a time, in a remote part of the kingdom of Langri-Shaan, a volcano began to erupt, throwing quantities of red-hot rocks into the air, and ejecting flows of lava that spread down the sides. The news was swiftly brought to King Nasheednezzar. After checking with some of his advisers, he ordered that the two villages located within some eight miles of the volcano be evacuated, and that all their inhabitants be safely billeted and cared for at royal expense in a town some ten miles distant from the volcano.

That evening he told the report to his Queen, the wise and beautiful Queen Kernizahde. "My dear," he said, "I know you are well informed about many things. Tell me a story about a volcano erupting, as it may have happened in that other world that we talked about from time to time."

Queen Kernizahde smiled; there was little she liked better than to tell stories. And so she said to the King smilingly, "My Lord, I hear and obey." And this was the story that she told.

In that other world there is an island in the Caribbean Sea which is called Martinique. On the northern half of that island there is a mountain called Mont Pelée, a volcano, which for several hundred years up to the year 1902 had been thought to be almost extinct. And there was a city of about 30,000 people called St. Pierre, located about five miles southwest of this mountain, on the seacoast. The last preceding "eruption" if one could call it that, in 1851, had produced only a cloud of fine ashes.

St. Pierre was a beautiful and rather rich city, full of charm and tropical flowers and trees, and many kinds of people. And the life lived there was in many ways calm and pleasant and unhurried, for the island grew rich crops and exchanged them for what the inhabitants needed from the rest of the world.

Early in April 1902, the year of this story, some persons who went for a picnic up on the mountain reported that they had found some new smoke holes that gave off sulphurous fumes.

During the next several weeks, the volcano rapidly grew more and more threatening. It made great noises like thunder; it produced two glowing craters; it sent up many clouds of smoke, ashes, and cinders illuminated with lightning; it spread sulphurous gases for miles around; it caused lakes up on the mountain to spill out of their basins, and pour down the slopes to the sea, cutting the roads that ran along the seacoast north of St. Pierre.

Toward the end of April, a lady who lived in St. Pierre, Mrs. Thomas T. Prentis, the wife of the American consul, wrote a letter to her sister in Melrose, Massachusetts, saying:

This morning the whole population of the city is on the alert and every eye is directed toward Mont Pelée, an extinct volcano. Everybody is afraid that the volcano has taken into its heart to burst forth and destroy the whole island. For several days the mountain has been sending forth flame, and immense quantities of lava are flowing down its sides. All the inhabitants are going up to see it. There is not a horse to be had on the island, those belonging to the natives being kept in readiness to leave at a moment's notice. Last Wednesday, which was April 23, we heard three distinct shocks. The first report was very loud; and the second and third were so great that the dishes were thrown from the shelves, and the house rocked.

We can see Mont Pelée from the rear windows of our house, and although it is fully four miles away, we can hear the roar of the fire and lava issuing from it. The city is covered with ashes, and clouds of smoke have been over our heads for the last five days. The smell of sulphur is so strong that horses on the streets stop and snort, and some of them, obliged to give up, drop in their harness, and die from suffocation. Many of the people are obliged to wear wet handkerchiefs over their faces to protect them from the strong fumes of sulphur. My husband assures me that there is no immediate danger, and when there is the least particle of danger we will leave the place. There is an American schooner, the 'R. J. Morse,' in the harbor, and she will remain here for at least two weeks. If the volcano becomes very bad we shall embark at once and go out to sea.

On May 4, which was a Sunday, another lady wrote to two relatives of hers in France, and said:

> I write under the gloomiest impressions, although I hope I exaggerate the situation. My husband laughs; but I can see that he is full of anxiety. He tells me to go. How can I go alone? The heat is suffocating. We cannot leave anything open, as the dust enters everywhere, burning our faces and eyes. All the crops are ruined. . . .
> My calmness astonishes me. I am awaiting the event tranquilly. My only suffering is from the dust, which penetrates everywhere even through closed doors and windows. We are all calm. Mamma is not a bit anxious. Edith alone is frightened. If death awaits us, there will be a numerous company to leave the world. Will it be fire or asphyxia? It will be what God wills. You will have our last thoughts. Tell brother Robert that we are still alive. This will, perhaps, be no longer true when this letter reaches you.

On May 5 one of the spilled lakes caused an avalanche of boiling water and mud to flow down a river just north of St. Pierre; this avalanche buried a sugar factory at the mouth of the river, and killed 150 people.

That same day, the French governor of the island, whose name was Mouttet, and his wife, moved in to St. Pierre from the other prominent Martinique town Fort-de-France, and stayed in St. Pierre, to "reassure" its inhabitants.

On May 6, a committee of experts appointed by Governor Mouttet studied the situation. They reported that nothing in Mont Pelée's activity so far "would justify the mass evacuation of the city." They also stated that the "relative position of the craters and valleys opening towards the sea lead to the conclusion that St. Pierre's safety is not endangered."

On the morning of May 7, an Italian ship from Naples was loading sugar in St. Pierre harbor. The captain of the ship, whose name was Leboffe, examined Mont Pelée carefully. Then he announced he was going to sail at once. In spite of protests from the shippers, and threats from St. Pierre port authorities to arrest him, he departed in his ship, saying, "I know nothing about Mont Pelée—but if Vesuvius were looking the way your volcano looks this morning, I would get out of Naples!"

On May 7, the editor of the local newspaper "Les Colonies" in his editorial published that day scolded those who had fled the town, and closed his editorial with the rhetorical question: "Where better off could one be than St. Pierre?"

Early on the morning of May 8, about half past six, a man named Ferdinand Clerc, a millionaire and mayor of one of the towns of Martinique, observed that the rumblings and internal explosions were louder and more frequent than they had been at any previous time; he also perceived that the barometer in his house fluttered violently. He decided to take no more chances with the volcano, and ordered his servants to harness mules to his carriage and make everything in readiness for flight. Meanwhile he had sent word to a considerable number of friends to come to his house. These he begged earnestly to leave as quickly as possible, but his advice was received with smiles and jokes about his great alarm. Immediately upon the arrival of the carriage at the door, Clerc put his wife and four children within and drove hastily away, leaving at his house about twenty-five friends whom he had advised to flee.

As he was driven rapidly through St. Pierre, he saw Mr. Prentis, the American Consul, standing with Mrs. Prentis at the gate in front of their house, gazing up at the column of smoke and fire that was pouring forth from the mountain top.

"You had better get out of here as quickly as you can," Clerc shouted to his friends as he passed them. "Oh, I don't think there is any danger," Mr. Prentis called back.

Mr. Clerc urged his mules on. When about six miles from the town he heard a tremendous explosion, and, looking back, saw, to his horror, a huge mass of gray smoke and ashes burst from Mount Pelée and fall upon St. Pierre. This was immediately followed by a jet of flame that rose a great distance in the air and seemed to topple over on the town.

What happened was this: on May 8 at 7:52 A.M., the flank of Mt. Pelée opened. An enormous thick black cloud of super-heated steam at a temperature of about 2000° Fahrenheit heavily loaded with fragments of hot lava, blew out horizontally. With a width of eleven degrees, the "Peléean cloud" traveled faster than five miles a minute. It blew almost south, directly into the town and harbor of St. Pierre, five miles from the point of origin. The cloud within two minutes destroyed the city—blasting, scorching, setting fires. All the people in the town—30,000 of them—were killed within a few seconds of the arrival of the cloud except for three persons only, who were found alive afterwards; and two of these died almost at once from their injuries. The third survivor was a prisoner in a jail, an old-fashioned dungeon with one small high window and one opening in the door, both covered with gratings. Although severely burned, he recovered. This survivor, whose name was Pierre Bachère, told the following story of what he saw, from the small grated window of his cell:

I was eating my breakfast that morning when the rumbling, which I had heard beneath my cell for three or four days previously, stopped suddenly. Then the whole place became black—a sort of violet black—and I heard screams all through the prison. I screamed to the jailers to come and unlock my cell, but I could not make anyone hear.

The little window in my cell looked out on the back of a convent, where 200 girls and a large number of nuns always were, but there was a high wall between my cell and the convent.

The violet darkness grew blacker and blacker until it was almost as dark as though it were night, and then suddenly the whole place was lighted up with a curious glow—sometimes red, sometimes green, but generally red. I put my little table against the cell window and, hanging on by the bars, attempted to look out, but I could not see anything because of the brick wall in front of me. While I looked, a huge red-hot stone crashed down just in front of my window, right on the top of the wall, knocking it down. The heat from this stone was most intense and made my post at the window fearful to endure, but the sight was such that I could not turn away.

Right in front of me where the brick wall had stood I saw the large convent, and I could see that molten matter had come down the hill and had run into the grounds of the convent. I realized then that there must have been an eruption of Mont Pélée.

To my horror I discovered that the lava had completely encircled the convent with its first rush and I realized that all the girls and Sisters who were in the building were doomed.

While I looked I saw another stone, even larger than the one which had fallen near my cell window and broken down the wall, strike the convent roof and crash through its three stories, evidently plunging through to the ground. I had not seen any of the Sisters until that time and I suppose they had depended for safety on the building, seeking shelter from the rain of hot ashes which I could see falling.

Scarcely a minute passed by after this huge stone crashed through when I saw the poor girls flocking out in utmost terror. Their actions looked as though they were screaming in an agony of fright, but I could not hear them at all because of the hissing of the lava and the roar of the volcanic eruption. As the girls came running out, I saw that they carried with them bodies of those who had been injured by the crashing of the stone through the building. Some they carried out were dead, while I could see that others were only injured.

The Sisters came running out, too, bringing appliances for helping the injured, but those who had hurried out of the building were driven in again by the blinding red-hot falling ashes and the fumes which I could see rise from the lava.

A pit had been dug on the inside of the wall in order that none of the girls should be able to climb up from the inside, and this acted as a sort of moat, in which the lava floated, and thus made a complete circle round the convent, rendering escape impossible, even if it had been possible to live in the rain of hot stones and ashes from the mountain.

Again, as I looked, I saw another stone fall upon the building, and this time more of the girls rushed out. A party of them broke down one of the doors, and holding this over their heads they tried to run for the gate, but were amazed to find their escape cut off by the river of lava.

The lava gradually rose and rose, and I could see the huddled group of girls growing smaller and smaller, as first one and then others succumbed to the poisonous fumes and the fearful heat of the surrounding lava. And as the group got smaller the lava rose and rose, until there was but a small piece of land around the building where the ground was not a heaving, swelling mass of molten matter.

Then with one great burst, it seemed to me, a fresh stream of lava flowed into the moat and overswept the building and the little island on which the girls were standing a moment before. I turned away my eyes in horror, and when next I looked nothing was to be seen of the convent but a heap of calcined stone, and here and there the blackened corpses of those who but a few moments before had been full of life and hope.

I could not see much of what was happening in the town for the reason that the window of my cell was so small. Besides there was a pall of blackness over all the scene. I could, however, see here and there as the smoke lifted that the lava had extended clear down to the sea and that only a few of the larger buildings had successfully withstood the attack of the volcanic eruption.

While I was looking from my cell window, my eyes almost seared out of my head by the heat pouring through the narrow orifice, I noticed a thin blue smoke curl along the ground, and caught by some eddying gust of wind, the fumes came straight into my cell window and I remember no more.

Mont Pelée was far from finished. A second exploding Peléean cloud on May 20 did considerably more damage to the ruins of St. Pierre, and there was a third such cloud in August. The result was that the territory formerly occupied by the city of St. Pierre lay uninhabited for many years.

"And that my Lord is a part of the story of Doomsday in St. Pierre, Martinique," said the Queen.

King Nasheednezzar: What a colossal tragedy!

Queen Kernizahde: So far as the people who lived there were concerned, the tragedy was avoidable. There was enough warning —for those who could heed it.

King: How many people accepted the warning of common sense and departed while there was still time?

Queen: The estimates are that perhaps a thousand left St. Pierre by sea or by land to go further away—in spite of the repeated assurances of safety. But these people were more than replaced by refugees who fled from villages nearer to Mont Pelée and crowded into St. Pierre.

King: I see again the time-honored pattern of human behavior in that other world: what people say to each other advocating inertia and procrastination outweighs all common sense, all glimmerings of wisdom. It would have been so easy for many more to just go further away like Leboffe and Clerc.

Queen: You are right, my Lord, in this case. But it may require much more than just a few added miles of distance to avoid other doomsdays.

If death awaits us, there will be a numerous company to leave the world.
                    —*A French woman in Martinique, May* 1902
I know nothing about Mont Pelée—but if Vesuvius were looking the way your volcano were looking this morning, I would leave Naples.
                              —*M. Leboffe, May* 1902

Fate leads the willing, drags the unwilling.
                              —*Cleanthes, c.* 250 B.C.
The fates stand in the way.
                                   —*Vergil,* 19 B.C.
'Tis fate that flings the dice, and as she flings
Of kings make peasants, and of peasants kings.
                                   —*John Dryden, c.* 1690
I am the master of my fate, I am the captain of my soul.
                              —*W. E. Henley, c.* 1903
Fate is unpenetrated causes.
                              —*R. W. Emerson,* 1860

Part VII

PROBLEM SOLVING

The Wolf and the Dog of Sherwood

AESOP AND E.C.B.

Once there was a lean and hungry Wolf who happened one day to overtake a plump and well-fed Dog, since both were traveling along the same highway. They fell into conversation, and the Wolf remarked admiringly how well the Dog looked.

The Dog, looking at the Wolf said, "You don't have to be so thin, my friend. Come home with me; my Master feeds his servants well; and he is looking for another one. And there is not much work."

The Wolf said, "That sounds very good to me." A few minutes later, having thought it over, the Wolf said, "All right, I'll come home with you and seek to enter your Master's service."

So the Wolf and the Dog trotted along together like friends; and visions of good meals danced in both their heads.

But soon the Wolf noticed curious bare patches all around the Dog's neck, where the fur was worn off.

"What are those bare patches on your neck?" said the Wolf.

"Oh, nothing much," said the Dog. "That's where my collar chafes."

"Collar?" exclaimed the Wolf.

"Yes," said the Dog. "Sometimes my master puts a collar on me and chains me up."

"Chains?" cried the Wolf in horror. "You never mentioned that side of the bargain," said the Wolf, shaking his head. "No— the woods for me." And so saying the Wolf departed.

The Wolf returned empty-handed to his lair in the forest of Sherwood, and there Mrs. Wolf suckling her four young cubs greeted him.

"What did you get for us to eat, my dear?" she asked.

"Nothing," said the Wolf glumly, "but I saved my independence." And he told her the story. She listened quietly to the end.

"Well, my dear," she said. "I am glad you saved your independence. But that does not bring us food. I do believe the hunting and gathering way of life is not a success any more. I have an idea. There may be a way for you to work for a Master without being tied up with a collar and chain.

"Why don't you go to the Shepherd over there," she pointed through the woods, "and tell him you now have a family to support, and apply to be an assistant to his Collie who guards his sheep. That flock of sheep is growing bigger and bigger. You can't do that job being tied up. You can only guard the sheep if you are not tied up. I know the Shepherd has a bad opinion of you—but tell him you now have a family to support, and ask him for just a chance to show what an excellent help you can be. You should be able to run faster and think better than that Collie; I know he is fatter and stupider than you are. And never, never, never bite any of the Shepherd's sheep!"

The Wolf said to his wife, "That sounds very good to me." He looked for a stick, tied a white cloth to it, and then set off to the Shepherd's hut, approaching it with his flag of truce.

The Shepherd called to his Collie, "Watch that thieving Wolf with both your eyes!"

The Wolf, arriving, said, "Sir Shepherd, please hear me out. Won't you please let bygones be bygones, and please hire me for a short while and give me a chance to prove to you that I can be useful as an assistant to your Collie to help herd your flock? I promise to serve you well. The reason I come to you now is that I have given up the hunting and gathering life, because I now have a wife and four cubs to feed, and I have to be a much better provider."

The Shepherd could hardly believe his ears. But, reflecting on this sudden change, he decided that the arrangement might be worth trying: he might change an old enemy into a passable friend; and he needed more help to herd his flock. Furthermore, the Collie was bigger and stronger than the Wolf; and it was desirable to have the Wolf visible all the time rather than hidden in the bushes.

So he said, "All right, Sir Wolf, I will try you."

The Shepherd tried him out, was well pleased with his herding sense and agility, and gave him good wages. And the Wolf family prospered.

E.C.B.

"What did you get for us to eat, my dear?" she asked. "Nothing," said the Wolf glumly, "but I saved my independence."
He might change an old enemy into a passable friend.
It was desirable to have the Wolf visible all the time, rather than hidden in the bushes.

We are so dazzled with the glare of a splendid appearance that we can hardly discern the inconveniences that attend it.
—Sir Roger L'Estrange, 1692
'Tis a comfort to have good meat and drink at command, and warm lodging, but he that sells his freedom for the cramming of his belly has but a hard bargain of it.
—Sir Roger L'Estrange, 1692
Paddle your own boat.
—Euripides, c. 440 B.C.
Whoso would be a man must be a nonconformist.
—R. W. Emerson, 1841
I was not born to be forced. I will breathe after my own fashion.
—H. D. Thoreau, 1849
All great alterations in human affairs are produced by compromise.
—Sydney Smith, c. 1845

The Three Earthworms

EDMUND C. BERKELEY

Once there were three earthworms that lived in wet black earth in a patch of field. Their names were Wiggle, Waggle, and Wobble.

From time to time, Wiggle, Waggle, and Wobble talked together about what it might be like aboveground, above the wet black earth where they lived. What was it like in that strange world aboveground—where there was no solid support for earthworms at all, and any earthworms who were occasionally flooded out of the earth promptly drowned in lakes at least ten earthworms across.

Wiggle said he just knew that the world aboveground was dangerous. Waggle said he just knew that aboveground was not as pleasant, comfortable, soft, and satisfying as the wet black earth in which they all lived. But Wobble said he was very curious about the world aboveground, and he intended to go aboveground and look for himself.

Wiggle and Waggle were horrified. Wiggle said, "It is very dangerous. Take my advice: be sensible and don't do it." Waggle said, "It is much better down here, in the wet black earth where we all live. Earthworms were not intended to live anywhere else. It is contrary to common sense to go aboveground, entirely outside the kind of life we are suited for. Take my advice: don't be silly—stay below." Wobble listened half-heartedly. Then he declared: "Well, I want to go, and I intend to go. Of course, I shall be careful, and I will come back." Wiggle and Waggle exchanged glances of the kind that said that Wobble was out of his mind.

Sometime later Wobble screwed up his courage, climbed up to the top of the black earth, where it was quite dry and rather uncomfortable, poked a hole through a clod of earth, and pushed his head out aboveground.

It was a clear and moonless night, with many stars. Wobble looked and looked and looked, and then he pulled himself down under the ground again.

Soon he came upon Wiggle and Waggle talking together, and he said to them, "Guess what I've done: I have been up to the top of the ground and looked out!" Wiggle and Waggle said with one voice, "Gee, what was it like?" Wobble said: "I saw something very strange. It looked like the inside of an enormous bowl, many many earthworms across, and there were hundreds of tiny holes in the bowl, and a very bright light was shining through from the other side." Wiggle said, "That is impossible. The world cannot be made that way." Waggle said, "Such a waste of time! You should certainly have stayed down in the wet black earth." Then they both told him nobody would believe him, and he had better not say anything to anybody for earthworms would think he was queer.

Wobble stayed down under the ground for quite a while. But his curiosity fermented inside of him, and finally it got the better of him, and he decided he had to go up aboveground and look again, and see what he could see.

When Wobble poked his head out aboveground this time, it was a little after sunrise on a hazy day. He saw a low sun and a hazy white sky.

An early bird saw Wobble, and came flying swiftly towards him. But Wobble noticed something coming towards him very fast, and he pulled himself down into the ground very quickly, just in time to avoid being caught by the early bird.

A little later he found Wiggle and Waggle, and told them that he had been aboveground once more. Wiggle and Waggle said, "Gee, what was it like this time?" Wobble said: "Again I saw the great big bowl over my head, but this time instead of being dark the bowl was white. Near one edge of the bowl there was a large, very round hole, and it was yellow orange and gleamed very brightly; and strangely enough, I did not see any pinpricks through the bowl at all." Wiggle and Waggle listened to him open-mouthed. Then Wiggle said: "How could it possibly be that what you saw this time was so utterly different from what you saw last time? Obviously, you are telling us lies, trying to make fools of us!" Waggle said, "You know if you tell lies to your friends, soon you won't have any."

Wobble did not say anything more. He could see he was wasting his breath, as well as losing his friends. But he was even more puzzled than he was the first time, and his curiosity welled up inside of him, so much so that he felt he would burst. Why indeed should the world aboveground be so different each of the two times that he had looked at it? Of course he was not lying to Wiggle. But it was very strange; Wiggle had pointed that out. Wobble said to himself, "I have to go and see some more."

For some time he stayed down in the wet black earth, and then at last he went up again aboveground, and looked again. This time it was noon of a bright summer's day; the sun was overhead; the sky was bright blue, there were no shadows, and it was hot, still, and very dry. He felt pain on his skin and in his eyes from the very bright light; so he stayed just long enough to have one good look all around; and then he pulled himself back under the ground, and rapidly went down to where the earth became dark and wet.

Wiggle and Waggle noticed that Wobble's skin was much reddened and thought that he might have gone up to the top of the ground again. So they came up to him, and said, "Well, tell us, Wobble, did you go aboveground once again?" Wobble looked at them and then he said, "Yes." They said to him, "Gee, what was it like this time?" He said, "This time I saw a bright blue bowl, with a big and exceedingly bright round white spot near the top of it. I could not look directly at the spot—for it hurt my eyes. Also, something or other pricked my skin, and now I feel very uncomfortable." Wiggle and Waggle listened with their mouths open. Then Wiggle said, "But it can't be like that. Why, that's different from both the ways you saw it before. That's impossible." And Waggle said, "You should have stayed down in the earth. Only the earth is the right place to live, right here in the wet, black earth which is home!" Wiggle remarked that the earth had recently been getting rather dry; and so they had all better dig lower in the earth to where it was damper and wetter. Wiggle and Waggle agreed that Wobble was crazier than ever, and telling them worse lies than before, and not worth listening to, in spite of the excitement of his stories. Talking together, they agreed it was simply impossible that the world aboveground could be so different at different times.

Wobble stopped arguing or discussing with Wiggle and Waggle. But Wobble's curiosity continued to increase so much that it actually hurt; he was so obsessed with wonder that he could hardly think about anything else. Time went by. Wobble no longer talked to Wiggle and Waggle about his three trips aboveground. But every now and then and finally quite often, when he could be inconspicuous, Wobble would go up aboveground and look around. Soon he managed to arrange for himself a little sheltered hiding place, an observatory, aboveground, so that he could really watch for a long time and see all that happened as time passed, in that strange world aboveground.

Then Wobble at last began to understand some of the mystery about the bowl, the pinpricks of light, and the great round blazing hot thing; he began to understand the changes between the dark bowl and the white bowl and the blue bowl; and he noticed that many of the changes followed rhythmically in multiples of about 50 earthworm time units; and so gradually he began to put together part of the story of day and night, and changes of the weather.

And so Wobble quenched his curiosity; and his whole life changed from restless, preoccupied, and unhappy, to cheerful, interested and happy.

But he never said a word any more to Wiggle and Waggle about his observations of the world aboveground. For he knew they would have told him that what he was reporting was impossible, that the world was not like that, that he was lying or crazy, and that he should have done as all good sensible worms do and stayed down in the wet black earth in the environment where it was ordained for all earthworms to live.

He intended to go and look for himself.
He had better not say anything to anybody for the earthworms would think he was queer.
His curiosity fermented inside of him.
It was simply impossible that the world aboveground should be so different at different times.
He was so obsessed with wonder that he could hardly think about anything else.
He should have done as all good sensible earthworms do, and stayed down in the wet black earth, in the environment in which it was ordained for all earthworms to live.

Seek, and you will find.

—*Mencius, c.* 300 B.C.

Search not too curiously lest you find trouble.
                              —*James Howell, 1659*
The whole is greater than the sum of all of its parts.
Half the truth is often a great lie.
The years teach much which the days never know.

The Hippopotamus and the Bricks

EDMUND C. BERKELEY

Towards the middle of the Tutulomlom River is a vast swamp full
of bulrushes and bamboos, cranes and crocodiles, and much more.
Here once upon a time there lived a Hippopotamus, who loved
the swamp, and loved even more the dark brown sloshy mud which
filled the swamp. The Hippopotamus loved to lie in the mud, play
in the mud, and to cover himself up in the mud with just his eyes
and his nose showing. And he loved to squeeze and squash the
mud to form it into many different kinds of shapes.

The shape that he liked most to make was the shape of a brick,
flat, wide, and long. He had once found a regular brick in the
swamp; he had carefully saved that brick, and he used it as a
model for all the other bricks that he made. He had also found a
split log that happened to have a good flat surface, and so he
could make very flat sides to his bricks. After he had made the
bricks, he set them out in the sun on a long, low ridge of rock at
one edge of the swamp. It was very sunny on the ledge and very
dry. The bright hot sun would make the bricks hard and solid.
But the Hippopotamus had no use for the bricks himself; he just
loved to make them. And being young and full of energy he made
stacks of them.

One day along came an Antelope. The Antelope was feeling unhappy—because most of the animals in the forest that surrounded
the swamp had homes—caves or burrows or nests or shelters of one
kind or another—but he, the Antelope, did not have anything reasonable like that. He had only a patch of bushes to call home. The
Antelope wanted a real home, not a pretend one.

He noticed the stacks of bricks on the ledge and stopped. He looked at them closely. He picked one up, turned it over and over, looked at the others, saw how nice and even they all were and an idea dawned in his mind: how nice it would be if he could just use those bricks to build himself a house. Then he would not have to live in a patch of bushes any more. If only he could take those bricks!

The Hippopotamus was watching the Antelope from a distance. He saw the Antelope admiring his bricks, and he sauntered over in the way that a Hippopotamus in the water would saunter.

"Mr. Hippopotamus," said the Antelope, "Do you know who made these wonderful bricks?"

The Hippopotamus felt as pleased as punch, and he said modestly, in a soft voice, "I made them."

The Antelope said, "You did? Well, they are very excellent bricks. What are you going to do with all those bricks?"

"Oh," said the Hippopotamus, "I don't really know what to do with them. I just make bricks for the fun of it."

"Oh!" said the Antelope, and he thought of another idea. "I think you are running out of space to stack your bricks. It's a pity."

"Yes," said Hippopotamus, "I don't know what I shall do."

"Well," said the Antelope, "I could help you. I can take some of those bricks away, and then you will have more room for some new bricks."

"Sure," said the Hippopotamus, "Take as many as you want. That will give me room for more bricks."

The next morning the Antelope came back hoping to obtain some more bricks. And sure enough, there were not only the stacks of bricks that he had left on the ledge yesterday, but there was a new stack of bricks which had just been made and which were in process of drying in the hot bright sun. The Antelope's mouth watered again as he looked at all the bricks.

The Hippopotamus was watching from the distance out of the corners of his eyes, pretending not to notice. But when he saw longing written all over the Antelope's face, he again sauntered over through the swampy water and said, "Well, Mr. Antelope, how did those bricks you took yesterday work out?"

"They are a splendid beginning for my new house," said the Antelope, and his longing showed even more plainly in the tone of his voice. "You know," he confessed, "I need some more bricks."

"Help yourself, Mr. Antelope, help yourself," said the Hippopotamus expansively and very pleased. "Those bricks are of no use to me. When I have played with the mud, and squeezed out the bricks, and set them in the sun to dry, I am finished. How could I use them in the swamp, I ask you? They would just melt back into mud."

The Antelope could barely believe his good fortune. That day and the next day and the day after that he carried away several loads of bricks, and the walls of his house grew higher and higher.

By and by a Zebra, who also needed a house, came by and noticed the fine brick house that the Antelope was building. Swishing flies away with his tail, he spoke to the Antelope eagerly.

"My good friend, Mr. Antelope, that is certainly a grand house you are making. And those bricks! Where did you get all those fine bricks? They must have cost a fortune, and excuse me for asking —how much did you pay for them?"

The Antelope said, "Well, can you believe it, there is a crazy hippopotamus down in the big swamp, and all he wants for fun in life is to make bricks. And—can you believe it—he has made so many bricks that he has to give them away to make room for more bricks that he is going to make. I am sure you can get some bricks for yourself if you want some, and I don't think they will cost anything."

The Zebra could hardly believe his ears, and hastened down to the drying ledge by the swamp and he called out to the Hippopotamus, "Mr. Hippopotamus, I have just heard about your brickmaking. Could I please have some of your wonderful bricks?"

"Of course," the Hippopotamus said. The Zebra gathered all he could carry, and trotted off.

Some of the forest animals, and especially the Lion who enjoyed the largest and roomiest cave for many miles around, made some very nasty remarks about the brick houses that the Antelope and the Zebra were making for themselves.

But the Antelope and the Zebra did not care. And many of the other animals who were using the bricks to make new homes or to remodel old ones did not care either. Day after day the Hippopotamus worked harder and harder to keep up with the demand. Finally, there were no bricks at all in the stockpile, and several animals would sit around, each laying claim to the next fresh unbaked brick that the Hippopotamus would bring to the drying ledge.

At last a day came when the Hippopotamus said to himself, "This isn't fun any more. I have to work too hard. I am tired. I am going to stop."

But the Antelope, who was making an extension to his house, and the Zebra, who was making a yard for his house, and the other animals who were graduating from old burrows and ramshackle shelters, all came to the edge of the drying rock at the edge of the swamp, and pleaded with the Hippopotamus and flattered him.

"Mr. Hippopotamus," they said, "even if you don't enjoy making the bricks any more, just think of all your good friends who have been relying on your excellent and useful bricks to build so much that is worthwhile. Won't you be kind and generous and thoughtful to all your good friends, and make us some more bricks? Mr. Hippopotamus, we need you. We think you are the finest Hippopotamus in the whole wide world. Please . . . please . . . please," said all the animals.

The Hippopotamus sloshed some mud over himself as he listened to this petitioning and then sloshed some water over himself to wash off the mud. Then he replied, "Well, yes, since you put it that way, I will work harder, I will try to increase brick production, I want to be kind to you animals."

After some months, he became extremely tired from making all those bricks. He said to the animals, "You know, I think you should give me something for making all those bricks."

So the animals looked around in the forest, and they brought him things. They gathered all the stuff they could not themselves use: dead wood; leaves that had fallen last year; acorn husks; old bones; snail shells; and rocks. And they stacked up a great big heap of stuff for the Hippopotamus. The Hippopotamus looked at all this stuff, and he said to himself, "Well, maybe it will come in handy sometime—and besides it was nice of the animals to bring all this stuff to me." So he kept on making bricks for the animals in return for the stuff they brought him.

But after another long while, there came a day when the Hippopotamus sat down and really looked over the big pile of stuff. Then he went nearer and looked closely at the dead wood; last year's leaves; the acorn husks; the old bones; the snail shells; and the rocks. He decided that he could not use any of this stuff at all. And he said to himself, "Why in the world have I made bricks all this time for junk, for junk, for junk? I can't understand what I have gotten myself into."

So he decided to go consult a wise old Crocodile who lived at the far end of the Swamp. He went to the Crocodile's area of the swamp and looked for him and found him lying on a bank under a big tree and looking for all the world like a great log, but ready to trap something small that came too near his large jaws. The Hippopotamus said politely, "Mr. Crocodile, you are wise, and I have a problem to consult you on. Can you tell me why these many months I have been making mud bricks in return for junk —worthless, useless junk?"

The Crocodile opened his eyes and looked up at the Hippopotamus and he said, "Yes, I have heard about it. Now, think, Hippopotamus, think, try to think of the reason why, because after all you have done this, and the question is *why* you did it. Nobody else can come up with a reason for you." And then the Crocodile shut his eyes again and relaxed.

So the Hippopotamus rested in the mud nearby and tried to think. He thought over all that had happened; an hour passed. Finally, he spoke again to the Crocodile. "It was this way, Mr. Crocodile," he said. "First, I made the bricks because it was fun. Second, I made bricks to be kind to the animals. Third, I thought I made bricks because the animals actually brought me something in return for them. But really, I still made the bricks because it was fun and because I wanted to be kind. And now I have done so much brick-making that I am really tired, and I have looked over the stuff they have brought me. It just isn't any use to me at all. This is what has happened. Now, what shall I do? What shall I do?"

The Crocodile opened his eyes and said, "Well, Hippopotamus, you have been making a mistake. It was hardly any mistake at all when you started, but it grew a little bigger and a little bigger all these many months you have been making bricks in return for junk; and now the mistake shows itself big and clear in front of your eyes. So you have to change, do some things differently."

The Hippopotamus said, "What?" The Crocodile said, "Oh Hippopotamus, the solution is simple. If what the animals bring you is of no use to you, don't make any more bricks for them. Just stop. Yes, I know it won't be much fun not to make bricks—but you can catch up on sleep and swimming and exercise and visiting and all of the other things that you have been missing while you spent all your time making bricks. And after you stop, some interesting things will happen." The Hippopotamus said, "What will happen?" The Crocodile said, "Let's see."

The Hippopotamus thought about what the Crocodile said. The more he thought about it, the more convinced he was that the Crocodile had a good idea. So he thanked the Crocodile and sloshed back to his own usual area in the swamp, and there he lay down in the beautiful mud that he loved so much, sloshed muddy water over himself, chased away the flies, shut his eyes, relaxed, and fell asleep—right in the middle of a workday and very comfortably!

By and by some of the animals came to the drying ledge, and found no bricks, and called to him that they wanted some more bricks. But the Hippopotamus slept and slept. More animals came, and there was louder and louder shouting. But the Hippopotamus was really tired. He had made a satisfying decision, and he slept soundly. After a long while, he awakened, heard the clamoring, and sauntered over to the ledge. The animals shouted they wanted more bricks, and called him lazy and irresponsible. But the Hippopotamus calmly said to them all, "My friends, I've decided not to make bricks any more. I'm tired. I've done it long enough. I don't want to make them any more. I have stopped. I have finished."

The Zebra shouted, "But you can't do that to us. Look, the Antelope and I and all of us are in the middle of building the finest brick mansions you ever saw; and we must have more bricks. Besides, look at all that good stuff we have brought you—why, those dead leaves from last autumn's leaf fall will make splendid rich black earth for growing things in. It will only take three or four years to make rich earth out of last year's leaves."

"That may be," said the Hippopotamus, "but I can't use the stuff. I don't grow plants, and I don't want to wait three years. I don't make fires and I can't use dead wood. I can't imagine how to use acorn husks, or old bones, or snail shells, or rocks. Who could possibly want rocks in a swamp? For me, the stuff you have brought me is junk. And my consultant the Crocodile has advised me: 'You should not make bricks in return for junk.' I have tried it for a long time now, and I'm tired. I am not going to do it anymore." And the Hippopotamus shut his eyes and submerged in the muddy water.

So the animals went sadly away and they thought and talked.

Finally they returned to the drying ledge and they called him. The Zebra said, "Mr. Hippopotamus, please, let's discuss. Item 1: We need bricks. Item 2: If what we have brought you doesn't please you, we'll bring you things that really do please you."

The Hippopotamus pricked up his ears at that. "Ha, ha" he said to himself. Out loud he said, "What would you bring me?"

The Zebra said, "Tell us what you would really like."

The Hippopotamus reflected, and then he said, "Well, I would like young bamboo shoots and the fruits of the mango tree, and wild asparagus and acorns instead of husks. . . ." He gave them a long list of tidbits and foods he would really like to eat. "After all," he said, "I am a big animal: I have to eat a lot every day, just to keep myself going."

So the animals brought him young bamboo shoots and mango fruits, and wild asparagus and acorns and other good things to eat. The Hippopotamus was well pleased.

He went back to making bricks out of mud. He put them in the sun on the drying ledge, and they became firm and hard. The animals carried the bricks away and in return brought delicious food to the Hippopotamus.

And the Hippopotamus said to himself, "I must remember— too much of a good thing may make it into a bad thing."

You have been making a mistake. It was hardly any mistake at all when you started, but it grew a little bigger and a little bigger all these many months. And now the mistake shows itself big and clear in front of your eyes.

He had made a satisfying decision and he slept soundly.

My consultant the Crocodile has advised me not to make bricks in return for junk.

I must remember: too much of a good thing may make it into a bad thing.

A fair exchange is no robbery.
                                   —*Tobias Smollett,* 1817
Everyone makes mistakes—that's why pencils have erasers.
                                   —*Alice Tilton,* 1944
Mistakes are often the best teachers.
                                   —*J. A. Froude,* 1860
The Blessed One preaches a middle path, avoiding extremes.
                                   —*Sakyamuni, c.* 500 B.C.
Don't be trapped by the precept "Be kind to the animals."
Praise and thanks may be sweet to one's ears, but true gratefulness
    has some substance to it.
Something repeated and repeated and repeated changes its character.

The Cricket Who Made Music All Summer

JEAN DE LA FONTAINE AND E.C.B.

A cricket who had made music all summer found herself extremely hungry when the cold autumn winds came. Not one solitary little piece of worm or of fly could she find to eat.

She went begging for some grains of wheat to the house of her neighbor, the ant, asking her to lend her some wheat until the new season.

"I will pay you," the cricket said, "before August, on the honor of a cricket, both principal and interest."

But the ant does not lend; and that is her least vice.

"What did you do in the warm weather?" said the ant to the cricket.

"Night and day, for all comers, I made music, lovely music— may it please you."

"You made music, did you?" said the ant. "I am so glad. All right, dance now."

❧❦

The cricket, who had been absorbed in her music all summer, was angry; but she knew her anger would not bring her anything to eat.

Searching further for help, in the stubble of the autumn field, she came upon a large, hairy, brown and black caterpillar, and asked her for some food on promise of repayment.

The caterpillar said, "You don't need food. It is autumn now. It is time for you to stop eating, spin yourself a cocoon for the winter, go to sleep in a comfortable well-fitting case, and wake up in the spring to a new life. Watch what I do and copy me. It's easy."

The cricket said, "But it's not easy for me. I'm not made that way."

Searching further, the cricket found a large brown moth with tattered wings, and asked her for some food on promise of repayment.

The moth said, "You don't need food. It is autumn now. It is time for you to stop eating and die, as I shall promptly. I've laid my eggs. I've fulfilled my life. Watch what I do and copy me. It's easy."

The cricket said, "But I am not ready to die. Also, my music is important to me, and I want to keep on making music."

"Well," said the moth, "perhaps you can use something I can't use, light and heat. See that woodcutter's cottage over there. I singed my wings there not long ago. Try over there."

The cricket eagerly made her way to the cottage, inconspicuously crossed the threshold, and took herself to the side of the hearth where logs were piled. There among the logs, she found a warm cranny, and some grubs to eat. Then, warm, fed, and happy at last, she began to make her music again, "Cree, cree . . . cree, cree. . . ."

THE·FOX AND THE·GRAPES.

The woodcutter turned to his wife, and said, "Listen, we have a cricket on our hearth. Now we shall have good luck—and music as well." And he scattered some crumbs into the woodpile.

E. C. B.

Since you piped during the summer, now dance during the winter.
—*Aesop, c. 570* B.C.
They must hunger in frost that will not work in heat.
—*William Camden, 1870*
Music is said to be the rejoicing of the heart.
—*John Florio, 1578*
The man that hath no music in himself
Nor is not moved with concord of sweet sounds
Is fit for treasons, stratagems, and spoils.
—*Shakespeare, 1594*
What to one man is food to another is rank poison.
—*Lucretius, 45* B.C.
The high prize of life, the crowning fortune of a man, is to be born with a bias to some pursuit which finds him in employment and happiness.
—*R. W. Emerson, 1860*

The Fox of Mt. Etna and the Grapes

EDMUND C. BERKELEY

Once there was a Fox who lived on the lower slopes of Mt. Etna, the great volcano in Sicily. These slopes are extremely fertile;

the grapes that grow there may well be the most delicious in the world; and of all the farmers there, Farmer Mario was probably the best. And this Fox longed and longed for some of Farmer Mario's grapes. But they grew very high on arbors, and all the arbors were inside a vineyard with high walls. The Fox had a problem. Of course, the Fox of Mt. Etna had utterly no use for his famous ancestor, who leaping for grapes that he could not reach, called them sour, and went away.

The Fox decided that what he needed was Engineering Technology. So he went to a retired Engineer who lived on the slopes of Mt. Etna because he liked the balmy climate and the view of the Mediterranean Sea and the excitement of watching his instruments that measured the degree of sleeping or waking of Mt. Etna. The Fox put his problem before the Engineer.

The Engineer liked the Fox because the Fox had brought him a neat little Engineering Problem. He too was rather disgusted with the Fox's ancestor and the bad reputation that foxes had acquired for their dealings with grapes. So he said, "My friend, Brother Fox, what you need is a little stepladder of aluminum. I have just the thing." He went into his storeroom, brought it out and loaned it to the Fox.

The Fox carried the little stepladder of aluminum to the vineyard. It helped him get over the wall, and when he was underneath the grape arbor he could go up the stepladder and pick what he wanted.

The Fox was quite happy The system worked splendidly for several nights. But soon Farmer Mario noticed that some of his grapes were missing. Mario studied the tracks. "Ah-ha!" he said, "a Fox—a clever Fox—and he has a stepladder. I must put a stop to that." So Mario placed a high steel wire fence all around his vineyard.

The Fox returned to the Engineer to explain the new situation. The Engineer said, "How did you like the grapes?"

The Fox said, "They are surely the most delicious in the whole wide world."

"Did you pay the Farmer for them?"

"Yes," said the Fox. "I brought him a sackful of the best potash and nitrate fertilizer from high up on the volcano. But seemingly he did not notice it. And so he put up that high fence."

"Well, my friend, Brother Fox," said the Engineer, "what you need is climbing irons so you can climb right over the steel wire fence. I have just the thing." He went into his storeroom, brought out the climbing irons and loaned them to the Fox.

That night the Fox climbed over the fence with two sacks of fertilizer leaving them in front of the shed door so that Mario could not avoid seeing them. Then with his stepladder he reached up in the grape arbor and picked a portion of the delicious grapes.

The next morning Mario came to his vineyard. He noticed the two sacks of fertilizer against his shed door and said to himself, "What a stupid place for my hired man to leave fertilizer!" Then he saw fox tracks again and said, "Ah-ha, that Fox again. I'll have to watch tonight and see what happens."

So that night Farmer Mario started watching from the shed. But he fell fast asleep. About midnight the Fox brought three sacks of the best fertilizer he could find from high up on the volcano, leaned them against the shed door, helped himself to grapes, and away he went.

In the early morning, long before his hired man would report for work, Farmer Mario awakened. He was greatly surprised to find he could hardly push the shed door open because three sacks of fertilizer were leaning against it. Then he found the Fox's tracks, and only the Fox's tracks. Evidently the Fox had brought the fertilizer, which was an even greater surprise. He looked in his grape arbors and found something like a dozen bunches of grapes missing—far less in value than the three sacks of fertilizer.

"So," said Farmer Mario to himself, "that clever Fox is taking my grapes and in exchange brings me fertilizer. Well, well, well! In the same way bees take honey from my flowers and in exchange bring pollen so seeds will come. Well, well, well! All right, I'll take that steel wire fence down and save it from getting rusty."

So Farmer Mario was satisfied, and the Fox was satisfied, and the Engineer was satisfied, and they all continued to live together on Mt. Etna—each in his own way of life.

That clever Fox is taking my grapes and in exchange bringing me fertilizer. Well, well, well! In the same way bees take honey

from my flowers, and in exchange bring pollen so seeds will
   come.
So Farmer Mario was satisfied, and the Fox was satisfied, and the
   Engineer was satisfied, and they all continued to live together
   on Mt. Etna, each in his own way of life.

We must help one another; it is the law of nature.
                                        —A *French proverb*
Help him who helps you.
                          —*an unknown author, about* 2000 B.C.

The Mice of Cambridge in Council

AESOP AND E.C.B.

The Mice summoned a Council to decide how they might best
devise means of warning themselves of the approach of their great
enemy the Cat.

   Among the many plans suggested, the one that found most
favor was the proposal to tie a bell to the neck of the Cat, so that
the Mice, being warned by the sound of the tinkling, might run
away and hide themselves in their holes at his approach.

   But when the Mice further debated who among them should
"bell the Cat," there was no one found to do it.

   Finally a young Mouse, who was named Albert (after Albert
Einstein), and who had had a good education as an inconspicuous
listener and observer in the halls, lecture rooms, and dining rooms
of a famous institute of technology, stood up in Council.

Albert said, "I have a proposal. Instead of fastening the bell to the Cat, what we can do is install many little bells with accompanying treadles in the passageways the Cat may use. Each little bell will tinkle when the Cat steps on the treadle because the Cat is heavy. Yet the little bell will not tinkle when we Mice step on the treadle because we are light. I know how those devices are made. The plan that I propose has the advantage that we do not need to go anywhere near the Cat—all we need to do is install the devices at times when the Cat is nowhere nearby."

The Council listened with great interest and surprise. Then an old Mouse named Thuselah stood up in Council. Thuselah said, "I have never heard of the device of which this young Mouse speaks—and I have lived for a long time. I believe the device has never before been tried or I would have heard of it. I am certain that Aesop never knew of the device or he would have written his accounts differently. My friends, I am convinced that the device will not work reliably, and so it will increase our danger rather than reduce it. Furthermore, as a matter of principle, we should never be 'the first by whom the new is tried.' I recommend that we devote neither time nor resources to this fantastic scheme." There were other heated arguments from Old Mice opposing the new-fangled, untested device, unknown to Mice forefathers.

But after careful deliberation, in view of the dire need of warning of the Cat's approach, a majority of the Council voted to try Albert's plan—on a small scale of course. The Council voted to appropriate a small quantity of cheese and nuts for the purpose.

Under Albert's supervision some alarms and treadles were purchased and installed. The system worked splendidly, and was extended. Finally, many of the Old Mice admitted its success by saying that they had always been in favor of the idea: this was what they had really meant by the words "belling the Cat."

Thuselah however continued to say that no lasting good could come from the new system. However, all the young Mice noticed that his actions displayed full response to the warnings given by the tinkling bells, by running to his hole.

E.C.B.

The plan that I propose has the advantage that we do not need to
    go anywhere near the Cat.
I recommend that we devote neither time nor resources to this
    fantastic new scheme.

Be not the first by whom the new is tried
Nor yet the last to lay the old aside.

—Alexander Pope, 1709

Who ever caught anything with a naked hook?
Nothing venture, nothing win.

—Sir Charles Sedley, 1668

Brer Badger's Old Motor Car That Wouldn't Go

EDMUND C. BERKELEY

One sunny day in this century when motor cars were common and
all the animals had started driving (because it was so much easier
than walking or running)—on that sunny day, Brer Badger got up
about five o'clock in the morning and set off in his old motor car
to drive several hundred miles. Less than two hours had passed
when his motor coughed a couple of times and died. Brer Badger
coasted over to the side of the road and stopped. There was plenty
of gas in the gas tank; yet he could not start the motor again. He
got out and lifted the hood because he had seen other animals do
that, but nothing he saw there made any sense to him. There he
was, stuck by the side of the road.

Leaving the hood up as a signal of distress, he hailed a Bear who
was passing in a big red truck. They rode four miles back uphill to
the nearest garage, which was called the Hilltop Garage.

Although it was still early, Brer Fox was giving gasoline to cars and taking care of Car Problems.

Brer Badger said to the Fox, "Brother Fox, I am in trouble. My car is four miles down the road. Though I have plenty of gas, the motor coughed and died, and I could not start it again."

So Brer Fox got out the tow truck. Together they drove down the road, fastened a tow chain to Brer Badger's car, and pulled it back to the Hilltop Garage. Then Brer Fox investigated.

"I see what's wrong, Brer Badger," he said. "Your gas line is broken." He pointed to some long copper tubing in the motor. "I can fix that."

So Brer Fox looked in his storeroom for a coupling, fastened it tight to both ends of the broken gas line, told Brer Badger to get into the car and start the motor. Sure enough, the motor started at once. Brer Badger gratefully took out his wallet to pay Brer Fox.

"Wait a minute," said Brer Fox. "Let's find out why your gas line broke." And he examined further.

"I see what's wrong, Brer Badger," said Brer Fox. "Your gas line is too long; it shakes too much; it'll break again. I can fix that."

So Brer Fox looked for some friction tape and fastened the gas line to some of the rods under the hood in such a way that the gas line could no longer shake.

Brer Badger paid Brer Fox gratefully and away he went. And although Brer Badger drove that old car around for many more years, and had a number of car troubles, the gas line never broke again.

I see what's wrong, Brer Badger. I can fix that.

Experience is the most efficient teacher of all things.
—*Pliny*, A.D. 77

Experience joined with common sense
To mortals is a providence.
                    —*Matthew Green, 1737*
One thorn of experience is worth a whole wilderness of warning.
                    —*J. R. Lowell, 1870*
Prevention is so much better than healing.
                    —*Thomas Adams, 1630*
The wisdom of prevention is better than the wisdom of remedy.
Whenever a trouble occurs and is remedied, look once more to see
    whether that whole class of troubles can be permanently
    avoided by some reasonable procedure.

The First Climbing of the Highest Mountain in the World

SIR JOHN HUNT AND E.C.B.

Once upon a time, in the evening of a clear and shining day in late summer, King Nasheednezzar and Queen Kernizahde, together with a small group of the lords and ladies of their court, were sitting in the garden of the Inn of the Rosy Mist. This inn was located in a rugged part of their kingdom of Langri-Shaan in the Valley of the Rosy Mist, a valley which pointed straight toward the highest mountain in the kingdom, the Mountain of Eternal Peace.

The garden was full of flowering roses—red, pink, yellow, orange, scarlet, crimson—all of them blooming profusely and filling the evening air with perfume. And as they looked east down the Valley of the Rosy Mist, they could see the summit of their great mountain. It seemed to float like a cloud covered with eternal snow, and lighted with rosy orange light from the setting sun.

The King turned to his Queen, and said, "See the glorious afterglow on our great mountain? My dear, do tell us a story of mountain climbing."

The Queen looked at her husband, and said, "My Lord, in former days, you did some mountain climbing, didn't you?"

"Yes," he said, "when I was young. I climbed some low mountains and on one occasion a glacier. In fact, the fever of mountain climbing almost captured me. But before it could, duty called me to the throne and I have had to repress many of my desires to climb mountains ever since."

"I see," she said. "Well, my Lord, I will tell you a story about mountain climbing in that other world that we have discussed from time to time, the world which contains for its highest mountain, one called Mt. Everest in the range called the Himalayas.

"Before the days when I became Queen of this kingdom, I interviewed a great man whose name was Sir John Hunt. He was the leader of an expedition that for the first time in history climbed to the very top of Mt. Everest. And I will tell you part of the story of how he solved the problem of climbing this mountain, and what happened afterward. But the evening is too short for all the exciting details, which would fill a book—the account of how he and his group of mountaineers overcame obstacle after obstacle, carried up supplies and provisions, camped night after night higher and higher up the mountain, and finally climbed to the crest. That part of the tale must be for another time.

"And I will use his own words as he told it to me, because it is a classic of problem solving."

This is the story of how, on May 29, 1953, two men, both endowed with outstanding stamina and skill, inspired by an unflinching resolve, reached the top of Everest and came back unscathed to rejoin their comrades.

Yet this will not be the whole story, for the ascent of Everest was not the work of one day, nor even of those few anxious, unforgettable weeks last spring in which we prepared and climbed the mountain. It is, in fact, a tale of sustained and tenacious endeavor by many, over a long period of time.

Shortly after we had returned from Everest, some of us were interviewed by a party of students. One of them turned to me and asked: "What was the point of climbing Everest? Had you any material objective, or was it just some kind of madness?"

Some may wonder why it was that we, and those who were before us, went to try to climb Everest, and it may be as well that I should attempt to answer this question at the outset of the story.

To those looking for a material objective, there is no satisfactory answer, for there was indeed no desire for, nor expectation of, any material rewards. The Himalaya is a rich field for exploration and scientific research, but there are many regions equally profitable and less known than the close surroundings of Everest for those who want to break new ground or whose interests are scientific. In the course of the many efforts to climb that mountain, the area has become relatively well known; during most other expeditions many interests have been pursued aside from climbing. But these other interests have always been secondary to the basic aim of climbing the mountain. Moreover, one of the lessons learned from the past is that science and mountaineering do not readily mix; I was always sure that we must concentrate single-mindedly on the main purpose of getting up.

Nor is the question answered simply by a passion for climbing mountains. To those who do so the sport is, or should be, a source of happiness. We climb mountains because we like it. But I doubt whether any one of our party went to Everest this year expecting to enjoy the climbing as much as in the mountains nearer home. Mountaincraft acquired on more accessible peaks tends to suffer in the Himalaya from lack of stern testing; most of us had been to the Himalaya before and we knew that, even on minor expeditions, the technical climbing problems are fewer and less severe, and the actual amount of climbing opportunities in a given time much less than, for example, in the Alps.

Yet to solve a problem which has long resisted the skill and persistence of others is an irresistible magnet in every sphere of human activity. It was this urge to which Mallory alluded when he gave his apparently ingenuous reply to this same question: "Because it's there." It was Mallory, who disappeared with his companion Irvine high on the northeast ridge of Everest in 1924, during his third expedition to the mountain, and since his time many more seeking without success to reach the summit, who by their example spurred us to try where they had failed. The fact that Everest still remained unscaled despite so many onslaughts was certainly sufficient to tame in us any foolish optimism, yet we were encouraged, as others must have been before us, by the possession of a mounting sum of experience. The possibility of entering the unknown; the simple fact that it was the highest point on the world's surface—these things goaded us on. The problem aroused no invidious comparisons; it was intimate to us as a team and personal to each of us as individuals. There was the challenge, and we would lay aside all else to take it up.

What is the problem of Everest? What were the weapons with which the mountain had so long succeeded in holding at bay so many resolute men?

By the autumn of 1952, when we were preparing to tackle it, the nature of the undertaking had been largely exposed; indeed, in a sense it was almost solved, with only the last 1,000 feet unclimbed. It was romantic to suppose that some spell had been cast over the final keep, that a barrier had been reached at about 28,000 feet beyond which even such stout spirits as Norton, Smythe, Wyn Harris and Wager, Lambert and Tenzing could not pass. It might appear that the problem was confined to the breaking of this spell, the forcing of this invisible obstacle, a point in space comparable with the barrier of sound. Although perhaps true in a psychological sense, to follow this line of thought would be to give a totally false impression, just as it would be untrue to say that, with the climbing of the mountain this year, there is no further problem for future aspirants to reach the top. Others had gone before us to approximately the same height on opposite sides of the final peak, but they had not been turned back by any physical obstacle beyond their technical skill to surmount. The terrain was passable; in descriptive mountaineering jargon, "it would go." Some among this select band maintain that they could have gone farther but for lack of time. I will return to this point later; it is enough to say for the moment that they had been defeated by the cumulative effects of altitude, effects which had been telling both on them and on their supporting comrades from a much earlier stage.

There are three factors of awe-inspiring magnitude facing those who seek adventure among the highest peaks. They are this matter of vertical scale, the climatic conditions, and the climbing difficulties. Let us look at altitude first. . . .

Here then, in very general terms, were the three big factors comprising the problem of Everest, those of altitude, weather, and terrain. It was in a careful study of these, and their effect on successive expeditions through the years, that our preparatory planning and eventually the operational plan itself, had their source.

We were greatly inspired by the fact that many of the difficulties arising from these factors had already been mastered by others before us; but we were also aware that we should have to face up to them again in our turn, probably in altered circumstances and possibly in more difficult conditions.

Finally, we knew that in order to reach the top we must somehow avoid the situation arrived at hitherto by even the most skilled and determined of our predecessors, when two, or sometimes only one man, had struggled upward to within 1,000 feet of the goal, with insufficient reserve to reach it—or at any rate to arrive there and return to join their friends. To enter once more into the realm of romance, we had to pass beyond that enchanted barrier, dispersing beforehand any spell by which the mountain might hold the trespasser hostage forever in its icy grip.

Organizing a major expedition, whether it be to the Himalaya, the polar regions, or darkest Africa, is a formidable business. I have experience only of the first of these undertakings, but I can now sympathize deeply with those who have the cares of planning and preparing missions in other realms of adventure or research.

Imagine that you are charged with the task of fulfilling, in company with others, a long and exceptionally arduous task, in some remote and uninhabited corner of the earth's surface, where climatic conditions are extreme. The success of your mission depends primarily on the human factor, on the joint efforts of every man in your team, and failure—moral or physical—by even one or two of these would add immensely to its difficulties. You have the responsibility of seeking and selecting these men, in whom you are looking for a happy combination of qualities which are difficult to reconcile. You will not be able, in most cases at any rate, to test these qualities, at least in conditions comparable with those which will confront you—it is unlikely that you will even be acquainted with most of them beforehand. You have to ensure that the party is suitably clothed and equipped to carry out its job in the especially rigorous conditions, and that it takes with it all the tools it is likely to require for the job, bearing in mind that communications will be so extended, slow, and difficult that you must be entirely self-contained for the duration of your mission. Some of this equipment is highly specialized, and difficult questions of design and quantities have to be decided. Provisions have to be calculated for the whole period of your absence from civilization, and they must be carefully chosen; a diet must be established suitable to the climate and the nature of the work. All these numerous items of equipment and food must be ordered, many of them only after thorough testing under conditions as nearly as possible approximating those likely to be met. Arrangements must be made for packing, cataloguing and moving them, as well as the party, to the starting point in a distant land, and from that point onward by more primitive transport to the area of operations. Last but by no means least of these manifold headaches, and governing the whole enterprise, is the problem of financing it; it is your job to calculate the costs. To complete this picture, suppose that you are given a bare minimum of time to launch the expedition and that you take it on with the everpresent possibility of its being cancelled when the preparations are well under way. You also realize that it will be necessary for you to make provision for a second expedition to carry on in the event of failure. In such a predicament you would, I fancy, be inclined to think that you were faced with as tough an assignment as any you had ever undertaken or were ever likely to in the future.

This, at any rate, was my impression when on September 11, 1952, I received a telegram inviting me to take on the leadership of the British Expedition to Mount Everest in the spring of 1953.

We now entered upon a period of intense and exciting activity. A carefully co-ordinated timetable had been drawn up, designed to ensure that no item of preparatory work should be overlooked and that each event should be dovetailed into its neighbors; everything led up to the great moment when our baggage would be stowed aboard a ship at the beginning of our journey to India. I was able to gather the party for the first time on November 17th and from then onward we met together at intervals of about one month until the date of departure. It was at once obvious that here was a variety of talent to take care of all the paraphernalia which it was proposed to employ in our struggle with the mountain; responsibility for obtaining and finally for assembling the multifarious items of equipment and stores was smoothly decentralized among the party and our reserves. With the burden thus distributed on so many enthusiastic and capable shoulders, I experienced an immense feeling of relief; the tempo of our preparations would now gather momentum.

The Queen said, "Now between this part of his account and the next part is the detailed, adventurous story of how Mt. Everest was actually climbed to the summit."

What were the reasons for our success? How was it that we succeeded in getting to the top when so many others before us had failed to do so? I am adding the second question only to give what, in my mind, is the one reason transcending all others which explains the first. For I wish once again to pay tribute to the work of earlier expeditions.

The significance of all these other attempts is that, regardless of the height they reached, each one added to the mounting sum of experience, and this experience had to reach a certain total before the riddle could be solved. The building of this pyramid of experience was vital to the whole issue; only when it had attained a certain height was it within the power of any team of mountaineers to fashion its apex. Seen in this light, other expeditions did not fail; they made progress. They had reached this stage when we prepared to try again last winter. By that time, but not before, the defenses by which the mountain had so far withstood assault were well enough known; it only remained to study them and draw the right conclusions in order to launch yet one more party which would have every weapon—material and human—with which to do battle against Everest. We of the 1953 Everest Expedition are proud to share the glory with our predecessors.

Above all, and independent of their lessons, we were inspired by their example, their persistence, their spirit of quest, their determination that there should be no surrender. For this compelling urge to continue the struggle, we have above all else to thank the earliest Everest climbers.

With this just tribute to the past, I would link the names of those who served on the committees which launched these expeditions and of others who generously contributed the funds which, alone, made possible each successive enterprise.

Next in the order of events I would place sound, thorough, meticulously detailed planning. On Everest, the problems of organization assume the proportions of a military campaign; I make no apology for this comparison, or for the fact that we planned the ascent of Everest on these lines. It was thanks to this that we were able not only to foresee our needs in every detail—guided by previous experience provided by others, we judged aright—but to have constantly before us a clear program to carry out at every stage: the march-out; acclimatization; preparation of the Icefall; the first and second stages of the build-up; reconnaissance and preparation of the Lhotse Face; even in outline, the assault plan itself. These were the aims to be achieved by given dates, and achieve each and all of them we would, and did.

I would once more pay tribute not only to the excellence of our equipment but to the fact that it stood up to the severe testing on the mountain and did what was required of it. Those firms, those zealous hands both in England and abroad, which took such great pains to produce all we needed, which worked, often against time, to do this, and those who gave us financial support, they must also share the triumph.

Among the numerous items in our inventory, I would single out oxygen for special mention. Many of our material aids were of great importance; only this, in my opinion, was vital to success. In this department perhaps more than in any others, those who worked to satisfy our requirements had the hardest task of all, for time was so short. But for oxygen, without the much improved equipment which we were given, we should certainly not have got to the top.

Was it worth while? For us who took part in the venture, it was so beyond doubt. We have shared a high endeavor; we have witnessed scenes of beauty and grandeur; we have built up a lasting comradeship among ourselves and we have seen the fruits of that comradeship ripen into achievement. We shall not forget those moments of great living upon that mountain.

The story of the ascent of Everest is one of teamwork. If there is a deeper and more lasting message behind our venture than the mere ephemeral sensation of a physical feat, I believe this to be the value of comradeship and the many virtues which combine to create it. Comradeship, regardless of race or creed, is forged among high mountains, through the difficulties and dangers to which they expose those who aspire to climb them, the need to combine their efforts to attain their goal, the thrills of a great adventure shared together.

And what of others? Was it worth while for them too? I believe it may have been, if it is accepted that there is a need for adventure in the world we live in and provided, too, that it is realized that the adventure can be found in many spheres, not merely upon a mountain, and not necessarily physical. Ultimately, the justification for climbing Everest, if any justification is needed, will lie in the seeking of their "Everests" by others, stimulated by this event as we were inspired by others before us. From the response to the news of our success, not only in our own country and Commonwealth but also in many other lands, it seems clear that the zest for adventure is still alive everywhere. Before, during, and especially after the expedition, we received countless gifts and messages of good will and delight, in both prose and verse, from all over the world, from heads of governments and humble folk alike. Very many of these messages were sent by children and young people. The ascent of Everest seems to have stirred the spirit of adventure latent in every human breast.

King Nasheednezzar: That was a wonderful story. Who were the two men who climbed to the top of Everest?

Queen Kernizahde: The Tibetan, Tenzing, and the New Zealander, Sir Edmund Hillary. Since 1953, other expeditions have climbed Mt. Everest. But they were the first.

King: I wish I had been along.

Queen: I am glad you weren't, my Lord. You probably would not have lived through the struggle going up.

King: I expect that's true. I like especially Sir John Hunt's sagacious remark, "The significance of all the prior attempts was that each one added to the mounting sum of experience, and this experience had to reach a certain total before the riddle could be solved." Perhaps that remark may be the clue to the survival of human beings in our world—even though it seems clear to me that people in that other world will destroy themselves.

The story of the ascent of Everest is a tale of sustained and tenacious endeavor by many, over a long period of time.

To solve a problem which has long resisted the skill and persistence of others is an irresistible magnet in every sphere of human activity.

Many men seeking without success to reach the summit spurred us to try where they had failed.

The fact that the mountain remained unscaled despite so many onslaughts was certainly sufficient to tame in us any foolish optimism.

There was the challenge; and we would lay aside all else to take it up.

We knew that in order to reach the top we must somehow avoid the situation arrived at hitherto by even the most skilled and determined of our predecessors—insufficient reserve to reach it.

When we prepared to try again, the defenses by which the mountain had so far resisted assault were well enough known; it only remained to study them and draw the right conclusions.

Next in order of reasons for our success, I would place sound, thorough, meticulously detailed planning; thanks to this planning we were able to foresee our needs in every detail.

The story of the ascent of Everest is one of teamwork.

The zest for adventure is still alive everywhere.

Princess Merribelle and the Evening Star

EDMUND C. BERKELEY

Near a waterlily pond, nestled deep among vast tangles of berry-brambles and fern-fronds, was Elfin Land III. Elfin Land III was, and perhaps still is, one of many ancient kingdoms grown invisible over the centuries. In the era of Princess Merribelle the Castle Hrrungarr (pronounced "h-rr-oo-n-g-a-rr" where "rr" means the r is rolled on the tip of your tongue as in Scottish or French) had become invisible to human eyes. The castle was invisible; the gardens were invisible; and the Elves of the castle had vanished from the sight of man.

In the day of Princess Merribelle, the waterlily pond had been discovered only by bullfrogs, turtles, and dragonflies. A hundred feet away from the pond, at a low point in the Royal Gardens of Castle Hrrungarr, the Elfin People had built a well from which they drew water.

Once in the early autumn, when the Princess was about eight years old, she went down to the well with her Nurse Emylla, who was to draw some water for tea. As she watched her Nurse draw from the well, the Princess saw what she had not noticed before: a sparkling blue star close to the tops of the trees near where the Sun had set.

Princess Merribelle also saw the reflection of the star in the pail of water, and it scattered shining silver blue light and sequins where the water rippled.

"What is that lovely star?" she asked her Nurse.

Her Nurse, who knew all manner of rhymes and childhood wishing tunes, told the Princess, "That is the Evening Star shining in the treetops. He was once a Prince called Hesperus. His reflection is resting in the pail. That is a lucky sign. You must make a wish."

The little girl closed her eyes and sang the words and melody of her Nurse's teaching:

> Star that splashes,
> Twinkles, beams—
> Grant the wishes
> Of my dreams.

"And what are your dreams?" asked her Nurse.

"They're a secret," she told the Nurse. "You mustn't tell anyone. But I'll tell you, dear Nurse: the thing I want most is a friend. Do you think Prince Hesperus might be my friend?"

The next afternoon, just after sunset, the Princess wandered alone to the well. She leaned on the wall of the well and looked into the treetops. Close to the setting sun, she saw the star, her star, her prince.

She talked softly to the star and it twinkled and sparkled very brightly. The wind blew in the branches of the trees and she thought she heard a murmuring among the leaves that said softly, "I am Hesperus, Princess. I am Hesperus, Princess. I will be your friend, Princess. I will be your friend, Princess." She wasn't completely sure what she heard, but this was what it seemed to be. She went back that evening to the Castle quite excited; and she almost told her Nurse about it, but she didn't.

That night she awakened about midnight, sensing the presence of someone in her bedchamber. As she opened her eyes, she saw in her room what seemed like a little floating star, like the Evening Star. As she watched, it changed quickly into the figure of a tall, young, and handsome Elfin prince clad in star blue and gleaming with star light. He came up to her, knelt by the side of her bed, took her hand gently, and smiled into her eyes.

She said to him, "Who are you?"

He said, "I am Prince Hesperus, and I shall be your good friend, dear Princess Merribelle."

She said, "How do you know my name?"

He laughed and said, "Didn't you tell me this past evening?"

She said, "Are you real? Or am I dreaming?

He said, "As real as Elfin Land III, Princess Merribelle, my dear," and he smiled at her again, a friendly loving smile that she would never be able to forget.

Then, during the time of a deep breath, he changed back into a little floating star, and vanished, and the room was dark.

Full of happiness and contentment, she fell asleep again. In the morning she thought and thought about what had happened; finally, she concluded that it should be classified as a dream that was real.

Each late afternoon thereafter, if the sky was cloudless, the Princess went to the well and talked softly to her star, and it sparkled. She became convinced that the star could hear her, and fancied that the star would talk to her every once in a while. In her loneliness as an only child and a royal princess as well, she was convinced the star had become her first true friend; and that her wish had become real; and that Prince Hesperus would after a while visit her again in her dreams.

Gradually as the days shortened and the winter came nearer, the Princess, wrapped in a long gossamer scarf with her mittens pinned to her sleeves with dragonfly antennae, leaning over the wall of the well, noticed that her star was growing fainter and harder to see as he became more and more part of the sunset.

"Oh no, dear friend, Prince Hesperus," she whispered. "Do not leave me." And she listened and listened, hoping against hope, to hear some response. But none came. And in a week's time, her star had vanished altogether.

The Princess returned to the wall of the well each evening for three evenings after the star had disappeared, only to discover that her star was still gone. On the third evening, she returned to the Castle, pale and shaken. She refused tea; then she refused dinner; and then she went to bed where she remained through the next day and the day after.

Nurse Emylla became very worried. She reported all her fears to the King, the Princess's widowed father. King Durance of Elfin III, who had a great white beard, and a passion for control of everything around him, went into a deep rage. The mood of the entire court changed from contentment to jitters as the King paced the halls. On the fourth day of his daughter's illness, he was muttering to himself and deeply angry whenever anyone spoke to him.

At last, the King burst through one of the doors of the Royal Hall and entered the Cloistered Chamber of the Austere Gician. Many years ago this Elf, because of his great learning and forbidding demeanor, had been appointed Most Austere Magician and Logician to the Court of Elfin III, to his Royal Majesty, and to Castle Hrrungarr; but it was too much trouble to say all that, and now he was always called just the Austere Gician.

The Austere Gician was seated at a round mahogany table shaking a golden gourd and reciting incantations.

"Incantations! Spells! Charms! Bah!" the King roared. "Don't you know the Princess is ill? Don't you know she may be dying?"

The Austere Gician rose and bowed.

"Sire, my associates and I have never yet failed you in time of emergency. No one, no elf, no creature has ever escaped our crystal gazing or our incantations, be he subject, ally, or foe. We shall not fail you now. Speak, Mighty Monarch of the Blood Royal of Elfin III, long may Your Majesty reign, tell us what you would have us, your loyal servants, do."

"My daughter is ill," the King shouted. "I want you to find out who it is has made her ill, and then mete out to the culprit the most stringent punishment. I want you to make her well. I allow you one hour."

The King turned on his heel. Ermine cloak flowing and white beard streaming behind him, he stalked out of the Chamber.

Down the hall, passing two doors on the left, and then through the third door, the King entered the Laboratory of Science presided over by Lord Ewton, Royal Astronomer and Chief Scientist.

The Laboratory seemed empty.

"Lord Ewton!" shouted the King. "Where is Lord Ewton?"

At the far end of the room, a slender Elf arose from a table on which was a telescope, and came forward. He was old, thin, with a remarkably large bald head, and a long, sparse and wispy white beard. A pair of large spectacles in a frame of spider web was perched precariously on the end of his nose.

"Yes, Sire. Yes, Honorable and Mighty Sire, at your service, Sire, your humble servant, Royal Astronomer and Chief Scientist."

"Telescopes! Instruments! Measurements! Bah!" shouted the King. "Don't you know my daughter is ill? Don't you know she may be dying? I command you and your scientific associates to find out with your science and your research why she is ill and how to cure her illness. I allow you one hour."

He turned on his heel, went out of the room, and with a vigorous shove slammed the door behind him.

Fifty-nine minutes later, the Austere Gician and Lord Ewton knocked timidly at the door of the Royal Suite. His majesty's Royal Elfin Guard Number Two ushered them through the Royal Foyer into the Royal Court Room where the King was sitting on his throne.

"Well?" said the King as the two Elves stood deeply bowed before him. "Well? And what do you honorable and pontificating Elves propose?"

The Austere Gician, looking at the King, glancing sideways at Lord Ewton, and clearing his throat, spoke first.

"Your Majesty," he said. "Your Majesty, the Princess's illness is a most unfortunate occurrence."

"Do you think I don't know that?" shouted the King, his rising temper again coloring his checks a bright red.

The Austere Gician, clearing his throat again, said, "The guilty party is . . . Sire . . . is . . . oh dear, oh dear, dear me," said the Gician looking at the King's furious face; and he shook his golden gourd most unhappily.

"Yes?"

"The guilty party is—the Evening Star."

"Some scandal newspaper!" said the King through his clenched teeth. "I knew it! I could feel conspiracy and scandal seeping through the very walls of the Princess's bedchamber."

"No, Sire," spoke the Austere Gician, shaking his golden gourd most sadly. "The original. The Evening Star itself."

"You mean that star that sometimes hangs above the treetops in the evening, twinkling for all its worth?"

"Yes, Sire."

"And what do you propose to do about the Evening Star?"

"Sire, it's a most difficult problem. Your daughter considers it her friend, but it has, of course, at this time, disappeared. It's on its way to becoming the Morning Star. The only thing I believe that is open to us is to issue a decree, prohibit it from becoming the Morning Star upon pain of extinction, and direct it back towards evening appearance. We would use the long distance power of the First Elfin Dynasty—and that, as you know, Sire, is rather old and somewhat weak."

"I see. Do you think the star will respect the decree?"

"It is doubtful, Sire, very doubtful."

"Pronounce and issue the decree immediately! Hand it both to the Town Crier and the Court Crier and devote yourself and your associated spirits to the business of bringing the Evening Star back to the evening. And you, Lord Ewton, what have you learned from your researches?"

"Sire, we have learned that the disappearance of the Evening Star has created a dangerous condition of melancholia in your daughter."

"Do you think I don't know that?" snorted the King. "What is the cure?"

Lord Ewton cleared his throat, bowed, and shook his head sadly. "Sire, the only adequate cure, according to the researches of my associates and the lore of the Elfin Association for the Advancement of Science, is to bring back the Evening Star, which is not possible. In the absence of that, we must teach the Princess to adjust to the condition of being without it. The therapeutic adjustment will require many therapeutic sessions and many, many days. The best therapy is slow. By the end of many days, a little less than the synodical period of Venus which is 584 days, to be precise, the Morning Star, alas, will have returned to being the Evening Star; and the Princess in view of her tender age may have become thoroughly confused. Alas!"

The King realized the profound Elfin wisdom of Lord Ewton, Chief Scientist and Royal Astronomer. His anger melted into sadness; he fell silent; tears came to his eyes. Then, the royal courage and determination rapidly returning, he declared:

"The problem, according to both of you, appears insoluble. So, I will consider other possible solutions. You are dismissed."

While this was happening, Nurse Emylla was sitting by the Princess's bed from time to time anxiously looking at her ill ward,

and from time to time gazing out of the window towards the long white sandy road that ran by Castle Hrrungarr in a wide curve. In each direction one could look along the road a great distance. It was nearly always empty of people and quite often empty of Elves.

But as she gazed, to her surprise she saw in the distance the figure of a man walking along the road towards the castle. He was dressed in clothes of ancient style, orange and purple; and he wore a cloak of scarlet, fastened with a gleaming brooch around his neck. He was singing and he carried a mandolin on which he was strumming; but he was too far away for the Nurse to hear any of what he was singing.

She leaned out of the window and called to Royal Elfin Guard No. 5: "Look, a Troubadour is approaching—run tell the King at once. Maybe he can help the Princess."

Soon the Troubadour was walking along the part of the road nearest to the Castle. Strumming on his mandolin he sang sadly and melodiously:

> Time
> Drips seconds
> From the bowl
> Of my life;
>
> And death
> Ever beckons
> To put an end
> To my strife.

Once in a while he looked in the direction of the castle, but he showed no perception of it, for of course to him as a human being it remained invisible.

A sudden breeze from the Castle gardens blew a swirl of red rose petals on to the road. Like butterflies the petals fluttered around the ankles of the Troubadour. He interrupted his strumming, smiled, stooped down, picked up several of the fragrant rose petals, and smelled them. As he held them to his nose, looking to see whence they came, their Elfin perfume rendered visible to him the Castle of Hrrungarr.

He stopped in his tracks, astonished, his mouth open.

At this instant, King Durance, Nurse Emylla, the Austere

Gician, and Lord Ewton, one after the other, ran pell mell out of the castle gate, and approached the Troubadour. Seeing the ermine robe and jewelled crown of the first of the four Elves, he bowed deeply.

The King cried, "O Troubadour, my daughter, the Princess Merribelle, is very ill and we fear for her life. Can your lore, can your music, help her?"

"Sire," said the Troubadour, "I am Leal Merimedon, Wandering Minstrel. My mission is to be of help, but I do not know much about the art of healing."

The King said, "Enter Castle Hrrungarr, and we shall explain."

A short while later, Leal Merimedon escorted by Nurse Emylla entered the chamber of the Princess Merribelle. In her great four-poster bed, she looked small, thin, and frail; her face was sad and her eyes were closed. The Troubadour strummed a few chords on his mandolin. Princess Merribelle opened her eyes, and said, "That's nice—play some more. Who are you?"

The Troubadour knelt down by the side of her bed. "It is I, Princess, a troubadour. Pray tell me the trouble."

The Princess said, "I had a friend, but he is lost. He has left me. I do not know where he is because . . ." Tears came into her eyes. "Because he has no home," she wailed.

"No home?" said Leal Merimedon. "No home? And who is this friend, and how has it come to be that he has no home?"

"My friend is the Evening Star," she told the Troubadour. "His name is Hesperus. He is a Prince. He had a home above the tree-tops when I first saw him one evening. I talked to him after that, night after night. When I talked to him, he twinkled and sparkled, because he was listening. He listened because he liked what I said, and he liked what I said because he listened. And, Troubadour, I love him."

"And what happened to this friend you loved?"

"He faded away into the sunset, as elves fade away when they leave the elfin realms. He has faded away and he no longer has a home. He has become invisible to me, as I am invisible to human beings. He is lost to me." And more tears welled up in her eyes, and trickled down the sides of her face.

"What would the Evening Star's home look like?" asked the Troubadour. "What kind of place does he want to dwell in?"

"A place all blue and sparkling silver."

"How big?" asked the Troubadour.

"As big as this," she said, and made a little circle with her forefinger and her thumb.

"I see," said the Troubadour. "I see. Now that I know what your friend wants, perhaps I can build him a new home, so that he will never be lost from you again."

"How can you do that?" asked the Princess eagerly.

"I have an idea," said the Troubadour. "Now rest, sweet Princess, till I come back. I will come back soon."

The Troubadour sought out the Elfin Smith of Castle Hrrungarr. At last he found in a part of the Castle a remarkable smithy, filled with workbenches, tools, cupboards, shelves, presses, several anvils, and a small forge. The Elfin Smith, whose name was Phaestus, was a short, muscular elf, with grizzled black hair and beard, a cheerful smiling face, and penetrating eyes that looked straight at you.

The Troubadour said to the Smith, "Would you please make for the Princess a little round silver box, with star blue phosphorescent enamel and sequins that twinkle and sparkle?"

The Elfin Smith listened, and he took silver, and star blue, and phosphorescence, and enamel, and sequins. He worked quickly and skillfully, like a good workman with much common sense and vast experience. In an hour he had made just what the Troubadour asked for, and the Troubadour thanked him.

"If I may ask one question," said the Elfin Smith, "what will the Princess use this for?"

"It's a home for her friend, the Evening Star," said the Troubadour.

"Hm!" said the Smith, rubbing his bearded chin. "The Evening Star is more than a thousand miles away and is bigger than Castle Hrrungarr. I don't see how that little box can be a home for the Evening Star."

"That's how it seems to you," said the Troubadour.

As he walked through the corridors of the Castle returning towards the Princess's Royal Chamber, he encountered the Austere Gician, who said, "What's that you are carrying?"

"It's a home for the Evening Star," said the Troubadour.

"Impossible," said the Austere Gician. "Young man, the Evening Star is a celestial object—you know what that is, don't you?"

"Yes," said the Troubadour. "A celestial object is something in the sky or the heavens, to use the old words, and in outer space, to use the new words."

"So," said the Austere Gician, "by definition, all celestial objects stay, reside, remain in the heavens. That's logic. So what you have there cannot be a home for the Evening Star. Right?"

"So it seems to you," said the Troubadour, and continued to walk down the corridors of the Castle. As he turned a corner, he almost bumped into Lord Ewton, who said, "What's that you are carrying?"

"It's a home for the Evening Star," said the Troubadour.

"Impossible!" said Lord Ewton. "Young man, the Evening Star, which the ancient Greeks called Hesperus, is the same as the Morning Star, which they called Phosphorus, and which the ancient Romans called Lucifer, and all are the same as the planet Venus, which is a round ball seventy-seven hundred miles in diameter traveling in an orbit around the Sun. Right?"

"Yes," said the Troubadour.

"So," said Lord Ewton, "the planet Venus which was the Evening Star in the western sky a few weeks ago, has now shifted in orbit around the Sun, and has become the Morning Star in the eastern sky. And if you will only rise tomorrow morning a half hour before sunrise," the Elf took a deep breath and drew himself up proudly, "I, as Royal Astronomer of the Land of Elfin III, will be most pleased to show you the planet Venus shining in the eastern sky before dawn, in all its luminescent splendor. So," said Lord Ewton, "what you have there cannot be a home for the Evening Star—right?"

"So it seems to you," said the Troubadour, and continued down the corridors to the Princess's Royal Bedchamber where he knocked gently on the door.

Nurse Emylla said, "Come in," and the Troubadour entered. He brought over to the Princess the sparkling little silver box with star blue enamel and sequins.

The princess, lying in bed, opened her eyes, and looked at the box.

"This might be a home for your friend," said the Troubadour.

She looked at it, and she liked it, and she sat up in bed.

"Yes, yes, yes," she exclaimed with happiness, "a home for my friend, Prince Hesperus, the Evening Star." She took it in her hands. "Look how beautifully it shines!" And she hugged it.

The Princess turned to the Troubadour. "Dear Troubadour, I thank you."

She held out a wan little hand. "You may kiss my hand and you may play me some music." He took her little hand and kissed it. Then he strummed on his mandolin and sang sadly in a minor key:

> Time
> Drips seconds
> From the bowl
> Of my life;
>
> And death
> Ever beckons
> To put an end
> To my strife.

"That is a sad song," said the Princess. "Besides, elves do not die—they only fade away—and you have stopped me from fading away."

The next morning the Princess was playing happily on the floor of her royal chamber, while Nurse Emylla sat in a rocking chair sewing. The little silver box that was the home of the Evening Star was on a silken cushion, which had been placed on a doll's little four-poster bed close by the Princess.

The Troubadour came in to her chamber to see her. "O Troubadour," she cried, "my friend is at home in the little silver box."

"How do you know?" said the Troubadour.

"I had a dream in the night," she said. "In the dream Prince Hesperus told me he will stay there now all the time, for a long time. Look!" and she opened the box, and the inside of it gleamed with such brilliance that one could almost believe that a starry radiance dwelt in it.

"And I'll tell you a secret, dear Troubadour," she said. "In my dream, he kissed me!" and her face lighted up with happiness, and she sang softly;

> Star that flashes,
> Twinkles, beams—
> Evening Star
> Of my dreams!

Tears started to come into the eyes of the Troubadour, to see such happiness in the little girl. But he said matter-of-factly, "How long will your friend stay in his new home, sweet Princess?"

"Until he goes back to visiting in the evening sky above the tree-tops," she said.

Later in the Royal Court Room of the Castle, the Elfin King sitting on the Royal Throne talked to the Troubadour, who was taking his leave.

"Troubadour," said the King. "Know that you have the unending gratitude of the Royal House of Elfin III for making the Princess well again. What reward do you wish?"

"Sire," said the Troubadour, "only this I ask of you: a handful of red rose petals from the garden of Castle Hrrungarr. Then, whenever I need to see what is invisible, I shall smell that Elfin perfume of Hrrungarr caught in the rose petals and I shall see what men ordinarily cannot see."

"Your wish is granted," said the King. He turned to Royal Elfin Guard No. One. "Fill the pouch of the Troubadour with the finest red rose petals of the Castle gardens; and then see him to the road, and wish him grace and godspeed."

Then the King turned once more to the Troubadour. "Your choice is wise. Know that the rose petals have still another virtue. The day may come when you want help from Elves. Then smell the rose petals; utter the word Hrrungarr three times; and then call, 'Elfin III, come.' We shall hear you though you may be a thousand miles away, or farther still."

A little later, with his pouch full of Hrrungarr rose petals, the Troubadour stepped from the Garden on to the long, white, sandy road, and looked back at the Castle. Princess Merribelle leaned out of her window, waved a little white handkerchief, and blew him a kiss on her fingers. He waved back. Then the Castle vanished.

He strolled down the long, white, sandy road, strumming on his mandolin.

What analysis of this fable can be made from the point of view of the problem, the solution, and common sense?

In the situation here, common sense again means nonspecialized knowledge, alertness, initiative, adaptability, and intelligence. This could reasonably have been expected from each of the four main characters in this story who failed to solve the problem: the Nurse Emylla; the King; the Austere Gician; and Lord Ewton.

Nurse Emylla failed because she did not really try to use her head at all; she just referred the problem to higher authority.

The King failed because he tried to solve the problem only in terms of giving rather peremptory orders to other people, supposedly experts.

The Austere Gician failed because essentially he was satisfied with logic, based on what we may consider to be medieval beliefs.

Lord Ewton failed because he was satisfied with science, the science of psychiatry and the science of astronomy.

The Troubadour succeeded because he investigated carefully and quite experimentally the meaning behind Princess Merribelle's statements, in terms of her own concepts. Most of the solution was suggested to the Troubadour when she told him how big the Evening Star was (as big as the circle made by her thumb and forefinger). So he was able to interpret what she wanted into a symbolic or representative solution, rather than a real solution, a real adaptation to the real world. This symbolic solution was successful because it fitted perfectly with the beliefs and imagination of a particular little girl eight years old.

It is worth noting that even in the real world there exist problems that have no real solution at all, but only symbolic solutions. An example is the problem of living forever. A human being cannot have real immortality. He must settle for "symbolic" immortality—such as the immortality of Aristotle, who continues to "live on" in the minds of men centuries after his bodily death.

Be not proud because thou art learned; but discourse with the ignorant man as with the sage.

—*Ptah-Hotep, c. 3550* B.C.

You should keep learning as long as there is something you do not know.

—*Seneca,* A.D. *64*

How vain is learning unless intelligence go with it!
                              —*Stobaeus, c.* A.D. *400*
There are more things in heaven and earth, Horatio, than are
   dreamt of in your philosophy.
                              —*Shakespeare, 1601*
True knowledge is modest and wary; 'tis ignorance is bold and pre-
   suming.
                              —*J. Glanvill, 1661*
A little learning is a dangerous thing.
                              —*Alexander Pope, 1709*
Tim was so learned that he could name a Horse in nine Lan-
   guages: so ignorant that he bought a Cow to ride on.
                              —*Benjamin Franklin, 1750*
An investment in knowledge pays the best interest.
                              —*Benjamin Franklin, 1758*
We know accurately only when we know little; with knowledge
   doubt increases.
                              —*Goethe, c. 1825*
To be conscious that you are ignorant is a great step to knowledge.
                              —*Benjamin Disraeli, 1845*

The world is more complicated than most of our explanations and
   theories make it out to be.
What you think may be true and what is actually true may be far,
   far apart.
The correct expression of a problem may be markedly different
   from the first half dozen efforts to express the problem.
Half the work of producing an answer that is correct is in phras-
   ing the correct question.
A vast amount of time and effort is wasted in solving the wrong
   problems.
Always look for additional aspects of a problem: they may turn out
   to be significant. Always watch for signs and clues: be ready
   to take them into account. Always there are traps for the un-
   wary: don't fall into them.
Some problems do not have real solutions in the real world but
   only symbolic solutions or representational solutions.
Cultivate a tentative viewpoint.

Notes

Part I. The Condition of Man

Pandora and the Mysterious Box. This parable, considerably expanded from the ancient Greek myth, is from *Myths of Greece and Rome* by H. A. Guerber, "lecturer in mythology," published by the American Book Co. in 1893.

The Garden of Paradise. Hans Christian Andersen, Danish writer of over 160 fairy tales, lived 1805 to 1875.

His parable "The Garden of Paradise" expresses a Victorian version of sin. We in our day may well interpret "sin" neither as eating of the Tree of Knowledge nor as unsanctioned love of a man and a maid for each other, but in other more far reaching ways related to dwelling on a small and limited planet.

The History of the Doasyoulikes. In 1863, Charles Kingsley, English writer, poet, and author of more than thirty books, finished one of the most charming and profoundly entertaining of all stories for young people, "The Water Babies." Its hero is Tom, the chimney sweep, who becomes a waterbaby, and whose adventures of exploration and whose love for a little girl Ellie have enthralled millions of young people and grownups also.

Within the main story are many smaller stories, and one of these is the fable "The History of the Great and Famous Nation of the Doasyoulikes." It has been slightly adapted to suit the present setting.

The Locksmith and the Stranger. This originally appeared in 1958 in the magazine "Computers and Automation" as a part of an article on the social responsibility of computer scientists. It was later reprinted in "The Computer Revolution" by Edmund C. Berkeley, published by Doubleday and Co., New York, 1962.

The Elephant and the Donkey. James Reston is a famous reporter of *The New York Times* and an officer of the corporation that publishes it. This parable was published in *The Globe and Mail*, Toronto, Ontario, Canada, October 10, 1972.

Where that Superhighway Runs, There Used to Be a Cornfield. This story is a portion of "Talk with a Stranger" by Professor

Robert Redfield, who was a noted anthropologist, a teacher at the University of Chicago for more than thirty years, and a president of the American Anthropological Association. "Talk with a Stranger" was published as an Occasional Paper in 1958 by the Fund for the Republic.

Part II. On Flattery and Persuasion

The Crow and the Fox. This famous fable was originally told by Aesop. The present version is by Jean de La Fontaine, a famous French author and writer of fables, who lived 1621 to 1695.

The Visitor Who Got a Lot for Three Dollars. This story is from Fables in Slang, published in 1900 by George Ade, American author and dramatist. He lived 1866 to 1944, was a reporter on the "Chicago Record" from 1893 to 1900, and wrote over a dozen books and plays.

The Cuckoo and the Eagle. This fable is by Ivan A. Kriloff, author, poet, and librarian, who lived 1768 to 1844. He was the great national fabulist of Russia. He proved to be a master of invention, and he found abundant material in the life of Russia around him. His first collection of twenty-three fables was published in 1809.

Part III. On Perseverance and Resourcefulness

Robert Bruce King of Scotland and the Spider. This story is on the borderland between fable and anecdote. Robert Bruce, a Scottish noble, who lived 1274 to 1329, became King of Scotland after much fighting with the English. This version is from Tales of a Grandfather: Being the History of Scotland by Sir Walter Scott, Scottish poet and novelist, who lived 1771 to 1832. It is from an edition by Edwin Ginn, published by Ginn and Co., Boston, 1885.

Part IV. Behavior—Moral and Otherwise

A Small Wharf of Stones. This anecdote is taken from The Autobiography of Benjamin Franklin, American publisher, philosopher, and statesman, who lived 1706 to 1790. He was a great practitioner of common sense and wisdom; over and over again his achievements occurred because he was ready and willing to change his mind upon obtaining good evidence for doing so.

Much Obliged, Dear Lord. Fulton Oursler was a famous Roman Catholic priest, and author of more than a dozen books. This true story is from his book *Modern Parables* published by Doubleday and Co., Inc., in 1950. The book is dedicated to the lovely heroine of this true story, Anna Maria Cecily Sophia Virginia Avalon Thessalonians. In his preface, Oursler says: "The Oxford dictionary describes a parable as a 'fictitious narrative used to typify moral or spiritual relations.' With this definition I have a minor quarrel. Why must a parable be fictitious? No story in this book is fictitious, and yet I believe each one typifies 'moral and spiritual relations.' They are all true stories. . . . It has been said that life is stranger than fiction, and certainly these stories which appear weekly in more than one hundred representative newspapers prove the point abundantly. . . ."

Part V. The Problem of Truth

On Being a Reasonable Creature. This also is from *The Autobiography of Benjamin Franklin.* See above, "A Small Wharf of Stones."

The Golden Trumpets of Yap Yap. This is from a book *Dangerous Thoughts* by Mike Quin. He was a columnist for *The People's World,* a newspaper published in San Francisco in the late 1930's, which published Quin's book in 1940.

The Empty Column. Dr. William J. Wiswesser, a research chemist at Fort Detrick, Frederick, Md., received in 1970 the Exceptional Civilian Service Award of the U.S. Army in recognition of his developments of chemical notation. He wrote the parable "The Empty Column" originally in 1950, in order to persuade some committees of chemists that a new (and therefore of course unusual) chemical notation could be beneficial. The persuasion was not successful, however, until the advent many years later of computer search for chemical compounds. This need finally caused the adoption of a new standard notation for chemical compounds which showed their structure and was written in a single line, the "Wiswesser Line Notation." This notation has been adopted in at least half a dozen large libraries that search for chemical information.

The parable portrays a fictitious struggle between Arabic numerals and Roman numerals in the days of the Roman Empire. Actually there was a real struggle lasting more than 300 years for recognition of "the empty column" with a symbol. It required from about 1200 to about 1550 for people in Europe generally to realize that in writing numbers efficiently, a symbol was needed to mark a place in the decimal numeral which held nothing, i.e., a cipher or zero. In some European countries calculating in this way was forbidden by law, so that it had to be done in secret. Not until paper became plentiful in the 1500's did the new notation really win out; and soon after that the shapes of the ten decimal digits became standardized because of printing.

The Differences in Two Strains of Corn. This is from *Plants, Man, and Life,* by Edgar Anderson, an extremely interesting book on crop plants, human behavior, and science in general, which was first published in 1952. Anderson was a botanist and a highly regarded teacher, who spent many years at the Missouri Botanical Garden, St. Louis, Mo.

The Ocean of Truth. This beautiful allegory constitutes the words of Sir Isaac Newton, 1642 to 1727, English scientist and mathematician, on his deathbed.

Part VI. On Common Sense

The Wasps and the Honey-Pot. Sir Roger L'Estrange was an English pamphleteer, journalist, and translator who lived 1616 to 1704. He retold several hundred fables attributed to Aesop.

The Deceived Eagle. James Northcote was an English author and painter, who lived 1746 to 1831. He wrote many original fables and retold many old ones.

Doomsday in St. Pierre, Martinique. The story told by Queen Kernizahde includes actual letters and eyewitness accounts of the disaster, which are taken from: *The Burning of St. Pierre* by Frederick Royce, published in Chicago by Continental Publishing Co., 1902; and *The Destruction of St. Pierre, Martinique* by

J. Herbert Welch and H. E. Taylor, published in New York by
R. F. Fenno and Co., 1902.

Part VII. Problem Solving

The First Climbing of the Highest Mountain in the World. Sir
John Hunt was the leader of the English expedition of 1953 to
climb Mount Everest, which was the first expedition to attain the
summit of Everest. His book *The Ascent of Everest* (English
title), *The Conquest of Everest* (American title), is an intensely
interesting account of the difficulties and the successes.

Some Collections of Parables and Fables

Ade, George: *Fables in Slang, and More Fables in Slang*. New York, Dover Publications, 1960, 190 pp. (First published 1899 and 1900 by Herbert S. Stone & Co.)

Aesop: *A Hundred Fables of Aesop* from the English version of Sir Roger L'Estrange with Pictures by Percy J. Billinghurst and an Introduction by Kenneth Grahame. London, John Lane, The Bodley Head, 1903, 201 pp.

F., C. K.: *Flowers of Fable* from Northcote, Aesop, Croxall, Dodsley, Gay, La Fontaine, Lessing, Krasicki, Harder, Merrick, Cowper, etc. New York, Harper & Bros., 1847.

Gay, John: *Fables*. New York, White and Allen, 1883, 238 pp.

Komroff, Manuel: *The Great Fables*. New York: MacVeagh and Dial Press, 1928, 486 pp.

Leonard, William Ellery Channing: *Aesop and Hyssop*. Chicago, Open Court Publishing Co., 1912, 158 pp.

Northcote, James: *One Hundred Fables*, Original and Selected. London, Geo. Lawford, 1833, 2 volumes, 520 pp.

Oursler, Fulton: *Modern Parables*. Garden City, N.Y., Doubleday & Co., 1950, 153 pp.

Rhys, Ernest: *The Fables of Aesop and Others—An Anthology of the Fabulists of All Countries* (Everyman's Library, no. 657). New York, E. P. Dutton & Co., 1913, 1958, 231 pp.

Townsend, George Fyler: *Aesop's Fables* based on the translation of George Fyler Townsend in the 19th century, with an Introduction by Isaac Bashevis Singer. Garden City, N.Y., Doubleday & Co., 1968, 215 pp.